GOLF
MAGAZINE'S

Play Like a
PRO

Time
HOME ENTERTAINMENT

© 2013 Time Home
Entertainment Inc.

Published by
Time Home Entertainment Inc.
135 West 50th Street
New York, N.Y. 10020

ISBN 10: 1-60320-239-0
ISBN 13: 978-1-60320-239-8
Library of Congress Number:
2013942590

We welcome your comments and
suggestions about Time Home
Entertainment Inc. Books.

Please write to us at:
Time Home
Entertainment Inc. Books
Attention: Book Editors
P.O. Box 11016
Des Moines, IA 50336-1016

If you would like to order any of
our hardcover Collector's Edition
books, please call us at:
(800) 327-6388 (Monday
through Friday, 7 a.m.–8 p.m.
central time, or Saturday, 7 a.m.–
6 p.m. central time).

Design: Paul Ewen
Photography: Angus Murray

A SPORTS ILLUSTRATED PUBLICATION

GOLF

MAGAZINE'S

Play Like a
PRO

Master the Must-Have Moves from the Game's Top Players

Edited by David DeNunzio

with the Top 100 Teachers in America

GOLF
MAGAZINE
TOP 100
TEACHERS
IN AMERICA

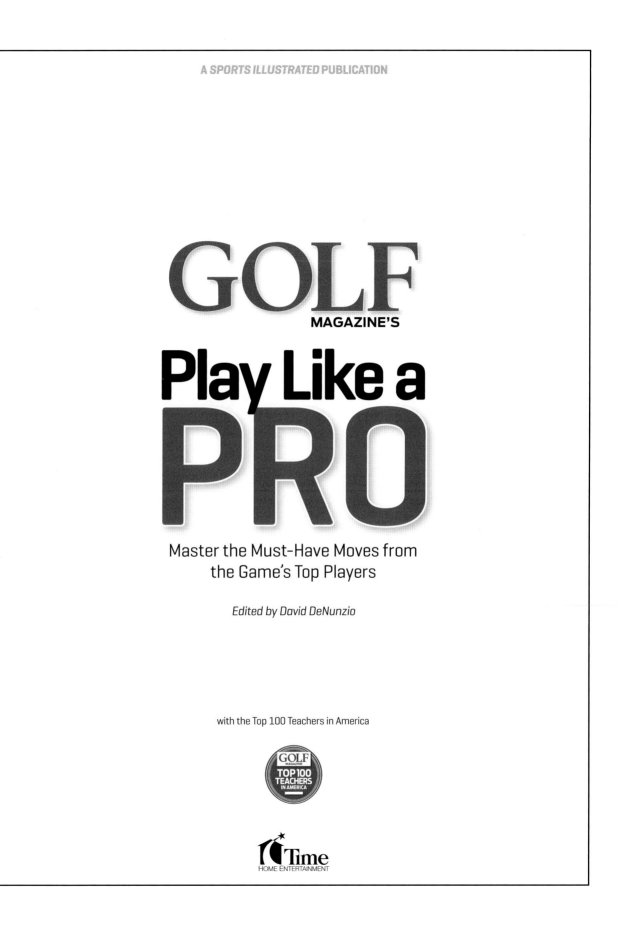

Time
HOME ENTERTAINMENT

Your Guide to the Greatest

Unlock the secrets to full-swing, short-game and putting mastery by

Hunter Mahan

Justin Rose

Section 1

Driving Skills   *p. 10*

● Don't just split every fairway. Split them with absolute bombs, using the proven skills of the Tour's fastest and most accurate drivers.

Section 2

Approach-Shot Skills   *p. 42*

● Bring every green into range and fire at any pin with the long-, mid- and short-iron swing keys from the most proficient ballstrikers of this generation.

Swings in the Game

copying the players who do it best on the PGA Tour

Charles Howell III

Adam Scott

Section 3

Short-Game Skills   *p. 80*

● Chip, pitch and lob it to tap-in range using the finesse setups and swings of the Tour's short-game and feel-shot savants.

Section 4

Full-Swing Skills   *p. 136*

● An in-depth, position-by-position guide to swinging your irons and woods with force and precision—just like your favorite players on Tour.

Get the Tour Touch

When you lace up your cleats for your Wednesday night company softball or rec league basketball game, rarely do you see yourself as your favorite MLBer or NBAer. And why should you? The skill set between the people who compete at sport—any sport—for a paycheck versus the rest of us is extremely wide. *Galactically* wide. When you're on the first tee at your home course or favorite muni, however, your target score—whether you can get there or not—is par. With "72" etched in your mind (or whatever happens to be par for the course you're playing), you're automatically judging yourself against the players on the PGA Tour, something you'd never do while participating in other athletic endeavors. It's both inspiring and unhealthy, and impossible to avoid because, let's face it, we all hit shots even Tiger Woods would be proud of now and then. Plus, the connection between amateur and professional is stronger in golf than in any other sport. Any week, you can walk right up to the ropes and get so close to Ernie Els that you can feel the ball compressing on his clubface. Try that the next time you go to the ballpark or arena. Security will escort you straight out the door. You can dress like your favorite Tour pro without the neighbors staring at you (like they would if you stepped out the front door in full NASCAR regalia), and if your pockets are deep enough, you can tee it up alongside a former Masters champion at a charity event. Sure enough, the line between pro and am in golf is often blurred.

If we're all just golfers (you, me, Rory McIlroy), then why can't we shoot the same scores? How do Tour players get to +6 indexes playing on the toughest courses in the world when you can't even break 80 on tracks that are more than 1,000 yards shorter? Practice plays a big part, so do the natural gifts owned by each and every card-carrying member of the PGA Tour. But there's more to it than that. Pros have the secrets—the closely held keys to full-swing and short-game success that the majority of golfers never get the chance to hear. That's where this book is going to come in handy. Inside you'll find all of the essential moves the best players in the world use in every part of their game to kick your swing out of the doldrums and get you shooting the best scores of your life. To help you understand the Tour's secrets and better put them into practice, we solicited the advice of *Golf Magazine's* Top 100 teachers to make sense of it all and further clarify right from wrong.

Can you learn from elite players? Absolutely—watching an ideal role model has been proven to accelerate improvement. Plus, if you're going to continue comparing your game with that of your favorite pro, you may as well start copying his moves. A brand-new, Tour-style you is just a few page turns away.

—David DeNunzio
Instruction Editor, *Golf Magazine*

The connection between amateur and professional is stronger in golf than in any other sport.

See It and Learn It!

Golf Magazine's **Play Like a Pro** is the first instruction manual with digital watermarks that, when scanned using your smartphone or tablet, deliver bonus content that brings the lessons in this book to life. More then 65 images are tagged, providing video tips from the Top 100 Teachers in America, pure slow-motion swing sequences and one-on-one lessons from the star players on the PGA Tour.

How to use the Scan-It/See-It digital feature in this book

1 Download and open the **Digimarc Discover** app on your smartphone or camera-ready tablet. It's free and available at the iTunes store for Apple devices and at the Google Play market for Android devices.

Videos also available at **golf.com/plap.**

2 Position the phone four to seven inches above any photo with a **SCAN THIS PHOTO** label (*example below*) as if you're about to take a picture. Use your device's camera flash if necessary. If you have access to a WI-FI connection, downloads will be faster.

Scan this photo *to watch a video of this lesson.*

3 Hold the camera steady for a second or two. The app will click and buzz when it recognizes the image and then begin downloading the described content directly to your device. Save your favorites for help when you're out on the course!

HOW IT WORKS

Invisible watermarks embedded in the page act as gateways to bonus content. With the Digimarc Discover app, your smartphone or tablet recognizes the watermarks and delivers the content (active until October 2015).

The average driving distance on the 2012 PGA Tour was 289 yards. In other words, if you drove the ball 289 yards, you were *average*. Decent, but not very impressive. The majority of weekend players are nowhere near this distance, despite technology that has made driving the ball easier than at any point in the history of the game. Flawed technique is certainly to blame, as is the discrepancy between the fitness levels of professionals and their amateur counterparts. And while it's almost certain you won't ever challenge Bubba Watson for the distance title, you can borrow his and his long-hitting peers' key moves to develop a faster swing. Even a slight improvement in your driving technique can give you the yards your game is missing and, if you pay close enough attention, the accuracy to drive the ball farther while keeping it in the fairway.

HOW TO PLAY LIKE...

- **Bubba Watson**
  Get his swing speed

- **Graeme McDowell**
  Get his accuracy

- **Dustin Johnson**
  Steal his power

- **Hunter Mahan**
  Learn his tee secrets

To use the Scan-It/See-It feature in this section, look for the SCAN boxes [*example below*]. For instructions, see page 9. Videos also available at golf.com/plap.

Scan this photo
to access bonus
videos and lessons.

PLAY LIKE A PRO

SECTION 1

DRIVING AND

TEE SHOTS

Bubba
Watson

Armed with a homemade swing that favors speed over everything else, high-flying and hard-hitting Bubba Watson proves that you don't need perfect mechanics to drive the ball deep down the fairway— just the ones that maximize the energy in your swing.

With a swing that tops 120 miles per hour, Bubba Watson is the new face of power golf.

SKILL BREAKDOWN

Scan this photo *for a one-on-one lesson with Bubba.*

"While parallel to the ground at the top has been talked about for decades, the greatest drivers in the world are almost always longer." —Brady Riggs

The modern game is all about distance. If you're missing a few miles per hour from your motion, then look no further than the current PGA poster child for speed and power, Bubba Watson.

Bubba swings fast, but he doesn't do it by simply moving his body parts faster. He creates a foundation for speed by tracing the widest swing arc possible. The bigger the width of your swing, the greater the potential to build up power. Bubba sets his big swing in motion by taking the club away with everything but his hands. **A wide, body-driven backswing like this can produce a great deal of power without any extra effort.** As he does this, he turns his upper body as far as his flexibility allows and gets the club way past parallel at the top. Who cares how far you take the club back? While parallel to the ground at the top has been talked about for decades, the greatest drivers in the world are almost always longer. Let your backswing stretch and stop worrying about how long it is.

In the end it's all about results. Bubba is not only concerned about outdriving everyone in the field, but also about shaping his shots. He's constantly making adjustments to hit different curves at different heights. Basically, he's playing golf with no concern about his swing. If you take the same approach, you'll not only enjoy the game more, you'll almost certainly play better. —*Top 100 Teacher Brady Riggs, Woodley Lakes G.C., Van Nuys, Calif.*

SKILL PRACTICE

1 Load up on your right side at the top.

2 Bump your left knee toward the target.

3 Straighten your left leg and "snap" into impact.

Scan this photo to watch a video of this lesson.

"Snap" Your Leg Straight for Bubba-like Speed

This simple drill teaches you to post up and slam the club into impact

By Top 100 Teacher SCOTT MUNROE, Nantucket G.C., Siasconset, Mass.

Unlike power-hitting Tour pros like Bubba Watson, you allow your left leg to slide ahead of the ball in a flexed position as you swing through the hitting zone, a move that causes you to lose a ton of power and clubhead speed along the way. My advice: Practice

hitting into an impact bag stuffed with lightweight material (so you can knock it forward when you strike it), following the steps at right. Use an iron, then transfer the feel to your driver. While it may not help you break the 300-yard barrier that Bubba cruises past week in and week out on Tour, it'll certainly help you speed up your swing and hit the longest drives of your career.

Step 1 Swing back while loading your weight onto your right leg. Stranding weight on your front leg during your backswing is a huge mistake that limits your power.

Step 2 On the way down, bump your left knee slightly toward the target as you begin to drop your arms. This will set you up for an explosive delivery.

Step 3 Through impact, rotate your left hip to the left while straightening your left leg, and do it without lifting your torso. It should feel as if your left leg—and the clubhead—are "snapping" into the bag. This move only works if you anchor your front foot to the ground. Immediately switch the bag for a ball and try to create the same sensation while hitting an actual shot.

SKILL ANALYSIS

Scan this photo to see Bubba's swing in pure slow motion.

Clubhead hovering above the ground at address. This guarantees a smooth and connected takeaway.

Long arms and minimal wrist hinge mean Bubba has moved the club with his body, not with his hands.

The true key to power: Transitioning from a wide backswing to a narrow downswing.

Pushing off the ground produces power and facilitates hitting up on the ball, a massive key for distance.

WATCH & LEARN HIT A JUMP SHOT FOR MORE YARDS

Golf fans have always had a love affair with long hitters, a fact that has helped Bubba Watson become one of the most popular players on Tour in recent years. His homemade swing, easy demeanor and shotmaking savvy are already the stuff of legend—Bubba is to driving what Seve Ballesteros was to the short game. His thoughts on his game run simple: "I know I'm swinging it well

when the ball goes far." In an age in which every Tour practice swing is digitally captured and analyzed down to the millisecond, Watson is certainly a breath of fresh air.

Bubba's 120-plus mph swing isn't one you can mimic overnight if at all. But if you're looking for a few extra yards on the tee, there are some Bubba moves you can borrow to make your swing

more athletic and dynamic. **First, copy Bubba's wide takeaway, and experiment with delaying your wrist hinge for as long as possible on the way back (frames 1–3).** That's an easy way to increase the width of your swing. Then, use more leg in your motion. Like most big hitters, Bubba increases the flex in his knees as he transitions from backswing to downswing, then straightens his lower

The width Bubba creates going back will translate into the most dynamic change of direction in golf.

Here comes the hinge. Bubba finally allows the weight of the club to fall as his body finishes the backswing.

Knees increase their flex. This is the squat before the jump that sends Bubba's swing speed off the charts.

Bubba is staying behind the ball and letting his arms and club pass his body through impact.

Still on back foot. This is allowed with the driver since it's the one club you use to hit up on the ball.

While this may not be the prettiest finish on Tour, it works.

---

body coming through impact. It's the same move you'd use to do a standing long jump. The greater the change in knee flex, the farther you'll jump—and the longer you'll hit it.

Look closely for these key moves in Bubba Watson's swing to help your driving game, but don't blink or you'll miss them.
—*Top 100 Teacher Brady Riggs*

Try This! | Squeeze Out the Speed

Place a car-wash sponge under your right arm at address. Imagine that the sponge is full of water. Hold the sponge with very light tension (so no water spills out) all the way up to the top of your backswing and all the way down to just before impact. As you reach impact, squeeze the sponge hard, so that every drop of water spills out. This gives you the feeling of saving precious energy until it's needed most.
—**Top 100 Teacher Jason Carbone**

Scan this photo *to watch a video of this lesson.*

Squeeze the sponge at impact.

STRAIGHT FROM THE SOURCE

Bubba on Bubba

"My goal on every swing is to stay in rhythm with the natural timing of my swing. It's something I've worked on a lot. Hitting good drives isn't all about swinging fast. It's about maintaining a rhythm so that everything happens in sequence. You don't want the clubface to be moving fast at the start of your downswing. You want it to reach top speed at the bottom. Although I'm proud of my distance stats, it's my GIR percentage that makes me smile. Hitting a lot of greens means I'm hitting a lot of short irons from the fairway on my approach shots. To get to this level, practice your sequence—lower body, arms, then clubhead—rather than trying to generate as much speed as possible."

HEAD

Notice how my head is way behind the contact point. I try to hang back like this while getting the energy from my body and swing moving toward the target.

HANDS

I rehinge my wrists almost immediately after impact as my body suddenly slows down and lets the clubhead whip through the ball. The leftover energy should easily bend your wrists after you make contact. If it doesn't, then your swing is out of sequence.

STANCE

Try setting up with an open stance. This allows you to move your hips faster at the start so they can lead your downswing. If you play for the resultant cut as I do, you'll hit the ball far and land it in the fairway all day long.

STATS & SPECS

Bubba vs. the Field

There's long and then there's Bubba long. Watson is 10 percent faster, and carries the ball 12 percent farther, than the PGA Tour average.

Stats from 2012 season; courtesy of PGATour.com

CLUBHEAD SPEED

Miles Per Hour

- Tour Avg. **113.0**
- Bubba **124.7**

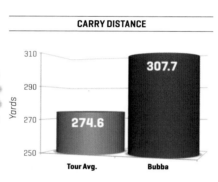

CARRY DISTANCE

Yards

- Tour Avg. **274.6**
- Bubba **307.7**

QUICK TIP

Keeping your head locked in place can block your upper body from turning as much as it can during your backswing. Allow it to swivel with your body to increase your rotation and coil.

Bubba's Blaster

PING G5

Loft 8.5 degrees (10 degrees open setting)
Swingweight D4
Grip PING 703-Gold
Shaft Grafalloy Bi-Matrix (X flex, 44.5 inches)
Tipping 0.5 inch

FEET

I ignore instruction that says to keep your feet glued to the ground. I like to feel like I'm pushing away from the turf, so much so that I get both of my heels off the ground. This is how I really ramp up my swing speed.

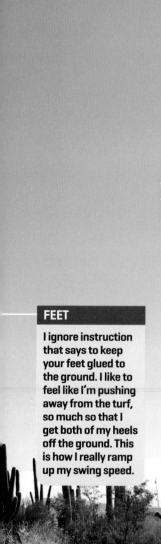

FINAL FIX

Look Up to Hit Up

Tilt your spine correctly at address for bigger hits

The key to maximum driving distance is hitting shots that launch high but have relatively low spin. To strike these types of drives, you need to hit the ball on an upswing, after the club reaches the bottom of its arc. To make this critical change in your technique, alter your setup position. Address the ball as you normally do, but instead of looking at the ball as you settle in, look up into the sky above your target. You should immediately notice that your right shoulder dips down below the level of your left and your spine tilts slightly to the right and away from the target as you shift your gaze up and to the left.

This is exactly the position you want when you hit your driver. Keep at it without reverting back to your faulty position. You should see a much higher ball flight and longer shots.

—*Top 100 Teacher Krista Dunton*

Scan this photo *to watch a video of this lesson.*

Yes! Spine correctly angled away from the target.

No! Spine straight or angled toward the target.

Since his U.S. Open victory at Pebble Beach in 2010, Graeme McDowell has found a greater percentage of fairways off the tee than nearly every one of his peers. His secret is using his body to square the clubface at impact instead of his hands and arms. He's a study in consistency and a role model for any golfer struggling with a hook or slice.

Graeme
McDowell

Graeme McDowell's body-squaring swing is a great one to copy for anyone with control problems off the tee.

SKILL BREAKDOWN

"McDowell's ability to split the fairway almost every time over the last few seasons is bordering on legendary." —Dr. Jim Suttie

Scan this photo *for a one-on-one lesson with G-Mac.*

Pro File

Graeme McDowell

Nickname G-Mac
Born July 30, 1979
Birthplace Portrush, Northern Ireland
Residence Orlando, Fla.
Height / Weight 5' 11" / 170 lbs.
College University of Alabama at Birmingham
Turned professional 2002
Professional victories 12 (2 PGA Tour)*
Majors 2010 U.S. Open*
Career U.S. earnings $9.1 million*

*Through 2013 U.S. Open

Rank File

European Tour Driving Accuracy		
2005	62.0%	[41st]
2006	61.3%	[61st]
2007	61.3%	[86th]
2008	64.5%	[37th]
2009	68.8%	[10th]

PGA Tour Driving Accuracy		
2010	67.1%	[48th]
2011	66.3%	[38th]
2012	70.1%	[5th]
2013	71.1%	[1st]*

*Through May 2013

Stats courtesy of PGATour.com

You need distance *and* accuracy to score your best. For the latter, look no further than 2010 U.S. Open Champion and Ryder Cup star, Graeme McDowell.

Whether it was born from countless rounds played on the windswept links of his native Northern Ireland or simply embedded in his DNA, McDowell's ability to split the fairway almost every time over the last few seasons is bordering on legendary. He's only moderately long by Tour standards, so accuracy for him is doubly important. McDowell doesn't mind hitting a longer iron into the green than the majority of his competitors as long as he's hitting from the short grass. He's smart—he'll leave the rough spots and tree troubles to the field. This is just one of the reasons why you see McDowell rise to the top in the most difficult setups.

His key? There are many, but **the main thing you can learn from McDowell is that it's easier to square up for impact using your body than by using your hands.** As you can see in the sequence on pages 24 and 25, McDowell noticeably bows his left wrist at the top of his swing. You might think this is a bad thing, but it actually requires him to use less hand and wrist action to square up for impact. Instead, McDowell employs a strong body turn, a move that requires a little more athleticism, but it's nonetheless easier to do on a consistent basis than manipulating the face back to square with difficult-to-time hand an arm action.

Big muscles are easier to control than the little ones. McDowell knows this, and that's why he's center cut on nearly every swing.
—*Top 100 Teacher Dr. Jim Suttie, TwinEagles, Naples, Fla., and Cog Hill Golf & C.C., Lemont, Ill.*

SKILL PRACTICE

Scan this photo to watch a video of this lesson.

1 Drop your hands straight down from your right shoulder.

2 Turn your left shoulder away from your chin. Don't move them together.

Once you reach the top, focus on three areas of separation.

3 Move your left knee toward the target while keeping your right knee flexed.

QUICK TIP
Pull your right foot back at address. This will keep your shoulders from opening too soon on your downswing and reduce your tendency to cut across the ball.

Separate Your Downswing to Stay on Plane

Use your body like Graeme McDowell for a power-rich and ultra-accurate inside delivery

By Top 100 Teacher MIKE PERPICH, RiverPines G.C., Johns Creek, Ga.

If you're a consistent slicer, your biggest mistake is starting your downswing using mostly your hands and arms, which causes the club to come down steeply and on an outside-in path. The trick to solving this problem is to take a page from Graeme McDowell's book and use more body to jumpstart your downswing. This will help you correct your sequence of moves so the club can attack the ball from the inside. To do so, focus on at least one of the key areas of separation shown above. (If you can do all three, great.) Work on the one that feels the most natural to you. By allowing these separations to happen, you'll give your arms enough time to fall onto the proper plane and deliver the club from the inside.

Separation 1 From the top, drop your hands straight down from your right shoulder. This will create space between the two and help get the club on plane.

Separation 2 Turn your left shoulder away from your chin as you start the club down. This will keep your head and body back and allow the club to swing through impact freely.

Separation 3 Keep the flex in both knees while getting your left knee moving toward the target instead of at the ball. If you do it right, you should feel a little bowlegged. This easy move helps your hips release to create extra speed and keep the club on plane.

SKILL ANALYSIS

Scan this photo to see G-Mac's swing in pure slow motion.

Erect address posture produces an outside takeaway. Not ideal, but it works for McDowell.

Clubhead outside the hands. This is ideal.

Perfect delivery plane, with the clubshaft on the right arm.

Right arm glued to the right hip at impact. This is perfect!

WATCH & LEARN GIVE YOUR DOWNSWING A HEAD START

Although it's highly accurate, Graeme McDowell's swing isn't that different from yours, making it the perfect model for you to copy for more consistency

McDowell isn't big (5' 11", 170 pounds). He isn't fast (112.8 mph swing speed), and his swing isn't what you'd call classic. That's good news, because it means you can find more fairways even if, like McDowell, you have a few quirks

in your motion. McDowell is too erect at address (just like most amateurs), he swings the club to the outside going back (another common amateur move), and he tends to lay the club off at the top. (You'll see this all day on any public range.) But check frames 8 to 10—he sets the club perfectly on plane. **He gets there by keeping his arms and hands quiet and methodically unwinding**

his lower body as soon as he transitions from backswing to downswing. It's this body turn—not anything he does with his hands and arms—that seemingly loops the club back on plane.

A good way to get this feeling is to make practice swings, but instead of waiting for your backswing to end before turning your lower body, rotate your hips to the left while you're still

Oops! Instead of continuing his turn, he lifts the club and lays it off. He'll have to reroute it.

Dropping the right elbow from the top gets the club back on plane.

Spine angle maintained all the way through the ball and club exiting out the left shoulder.

A balanced finish never goes out of style.

swinging the club back. Not only will you almost magically reroute the club for an inside delivery, you'll add some whip action to your swing and a few extra yards to boot. If you can make this important move at this crucial moment in your backswing, you'll stripe it regardless of what happens before or after.
—*Top 100 Teacher Brady Riggs*

Try This! | ## Put Your Pinkie on the Handle

Instead of placing your bottom hand on the club so that your pinkie is at the very end, or just off, the grip, try choking down a bit. You should use the heel pad of your left hand to guide your hand placement, making sure that the end of the grip actually protrudes from your hand. The best place to check this is at the top of your swing. Although a slightly shorter grip will likely make your swing feel a little shorter at the top, you'll actually have much more control over the club and will be able to hold it using less pressure.
—**Top 100 Teacher Todd Sones**

No!

Yes!

STRAIGHT FROM THE SOURCE

Graeme on Graeme

"On every tee box I decide if I'm going to play for position or for distance, depending on the obstacles I see. Once I make up my mind, I stick to my plan. Although my average swing speed is around 113 mph, I can swing faster than that, and certainly much slower. My goal on tight holes is to go after the ball at 85 percent of my maximum capacity. That allows me to strike the ball without producing a lot of curve. When I need to shift to a higher gear, I do everything the same, only faster. Regardless of how fast or slow I swing, I never deviate from my core swing keys."

LEFT ARM

I like to feel that the upper part of my left arm is tight against the left side of my chest from address until I hinge the club up in my through-swing. This connection ensures that your hands and arms won't race ahead or lag behind your body.

HIPS

Once I'm in the slot, I focus on getting my hips to face the target as soon as possible. It really helps if you focus on your core muscles and feel as if they're pulling everything through impact. This will help you remain in your posture, too.

PRACTICE

Find a way to catch the ball in the center of the clubface as opposed to near the heel or toe. You'll not only drive it straighter, you'll also hit it farther, because that's where maximum energy transfer takes place.

STATS & SPECS

McDowell vs. the Field

Graeme McDowell hits about six more fairways than the average PGA Tour pro over the course of a four-day event. When he does find the rough, he's 25 percent closer to the edge of the fairway than his competitors.

Stats from 2012 season; courtesy of PGATour.com

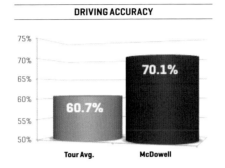

DRIVING ACCURACY

- 75%
- 70%
- 65%
- 60%
- 55%
- 50%

Tour Avg. **60.7%** — McDowell **70.1%**

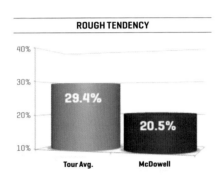

ROUGH TENDENCY

- 40%
- 30%
- 20%
- 10%

Tour Avg. **29.4%** — McDowell **20.5%**

G-Mac's Fairway Finder

Cleveland Classic 290
Loft 10.5 degrees (*stamped 9 degrees*)
Shaft Miyazaki Kusala Indigo 56 (*X flex, 46 inches*)

TEE

Teeing the ball lower is my way of making sure I hit the fairway at all costs. The lower tee height encourages me to hit down on the ball more, which automatically creates extra backspin, even with a low-lofted club like the driver

FINAL FIX

Build Accuracy at the Start

Step one is to stand the correct distance from the ball

Consistency in your swing starts with a consistent setup. Instead of simply going by feel, follow these simple steps to make sure you have the right amount of forward bend and to ensure you're the correct distance from the ball—two of the most damaging amateur setup errors.

Step 1 Assume your setup position with your driver and check where the butt of the club is pointing—it should be aimed at the center of your zipper. If it's pointing at your stomach you're standing up too tall, and if it's pointing at your inseam you're bent over too much.

Step 2 Now hold your position but take your right hand off the club and open it wide (*photo, right*). Use your open hand to measure the distance from the butt of the club to your legs. Get this distance correct every time and you'll know you're set up correctly for accurate hits.
—*Top 100 Teacher Jim Murphy*

Scan this photo *to watch a video of this lesson.*

You're set up correctly when the shaft points at your zipper and you can fit your open hand between the butt of the club and your legs.

Skill No. 3
SMASH FACTOR

Dustin Johnson's ability to translate swing speed into ball speed is the result of prioritizing contact on the center of the clubface over everything else.

Dustin
Johnson

Only a handful of big hitters get more ball speed per clubhead speed—smash factor—than the überathletic, megaflexible Dustin Johnson. Here's how he does it and the moves you can copy to make your driver swing not only more powerful, but also more efficient.

SKILL BREAKDOWN

The Smash Factor Address

STAND TALLER
Don't bend forward so much. You want to feel a slight curve in the small of your back and that your chin is up. This gives you the room you need to swing through impact without getting stuck.

FEEL THE HANG
Your upper arms should hang almost straight down. A line drawn along the shaft, through the grip and into your body should hit your belt buckle.

SPREAD YOUR WEIGHT
You should feel like an athlete ready to move in any direction. This can only happen if you center your weight. When you step into your setup, shuffle your feet slightly to move your weight evenly between both feet and evenly between your toes and heels.

Pro File

Dustin Johnson

Full name Dustin Hunter Johnson
Nickname D.J.
Born June 22, 1984
Birthplace Columbia, S.C.
Residence Jupiter, Fla.
Height / Weight 6' 4" / 190 lbs.
College Coastal Carolina University
Turned professional 2007
Professional victories 9 [7 PGA Tour]*
Majors None*
Career U.S. earnings $18.8 million*

*Through 2013 U.S. Open

Rank File

Efficient Power

Ball Speed
180.6 mph [4th]

Clubhead Speed
121.6 mph [5th]

Smash Factor
1.485 [3rd]

Driving Distance
310.2 yards [2nd]

Stats from 2012 season; courtesy of PGATour.com

D.J.'s Driver

TaylorMade R1

As you can guess, the ball rockets off the clubhead faster when contact is made on the sweet spot, and one of the best at doing this week in and week out on the PGA Tour is Dustin Johnson. The South Carolina native's smash factor, a value determined by dividing ball speed by clubhead speed, is nearly off the charts. The USGA has limited manufacturers from producing a face that delivers a smash factor more than 1.5. In 2012, Johnson averaged 1.485. In other words, Johnson's driving prowess is almost illegal.

His secret? Johnson is tall (6' 4"). He's athletic. (He can dunk a basketball.) And he has built a swing rife with speed and the ability to square up the face with alarming consistency. You'll learn how he does it on the following pages, but before delving into technique, it's important to understand that much of what Johnson is able to accomplish with his driver swing is a result of a picture-perfect setup. While the address position is likely the most mundane section of the swing to analyze and work on, it's nonetheless critical to putting your body in the correct position at the very start. **The likelihood of centered contact drops dramatically the more you deviate from the address basics proven to fuel an on-plane swing.** Copy what you see above and you'll make an immediate improvement in your ability to get more smash from your swing.
—*Top 100 Teacher Tom Stickney, Bighorn G.C., Palm Desert, Calif.*

SKILL PRACTICE

SLOW HERE

The only way for amateurs to hit successful shots is to make a slow transition. Don't start to crank up the speed until you deliver the club to the impact zone.

QUICK TIP
Point your right index finger down the right side of the grip and press it tightly against the handle. This makes it difficult for your swing to break down at the top and at impact.

FAST HERE

Swing Slow-to-Fast for Extra Smash

Add speed at the bottom of your swing instead of pouring it on from the top

By Top 100 Teacher CHARLIE KING, Reynolds Plantation Golf Academy, Greensboro, Ga.

In an effort to create extra power in your swing, especially when hitting driver, you take the club back very quickly and then make a rushed, herky-jerky transition into your downswing. The result is an out-of-control motion that produces inconsistent shots with poor accuracy and distance. That's not what powerful and efficient drivers such as Dustin Johnson do.

The secret to developing greater consistency in your ballstriking and improving the overall quality of your drives is to make a smooth transition from backswing to downswing every time you hit the ball. Smoothing your transition will not only help you make better contact; it will also help you create more power, because an overly fast transition is guaranteed to release your power far too early.

Take the club back at a moderate (not fast) pace and continue that same speed as you change direction and begin swinging the club down toward the ball. Don't crank up your swing to full speed until you're about halfway down. Remember, the goal on any swing is to reach maximum clubhead speed through impact, not well before it, and this technique will help you gain momentum gradually instead of using all your energy at the beginning of the downswing (where speed is meaningless). Think "slow at the top, fast at the bottom" and you'll have the right idea.

STRAIGHT FROM THE SOURCE

Dustin on Dustin

"I've always hit the ball far—at 6' 4" it's easy for me to generate speed—but I continue to pick up yards every season. One thing that allows me to swing fast yet consistently make contact in the center of the clubface is to minimize my angles and make a level turn through the ball.

On every driver swing, my goal is to remain standing tall so that my arms have enough room to come through and fire the club with max power. I lose the space I need when I start bending my knees on the way back down. This sets my shoulder line, my belt line and my knee line at too severe an angle, which makes it impossible to return to my address posture at impact (a good thing to think about to make consistently solid contact).

When I practice this move, I like to picture a circle on my right hip. As I turn from the top of my backswing, I think of keeping the circle at the same height and my knees stable. If I do it right, my hips will be level at impact and I'll have ample space to fire the clubhead through the ball."

DO THIS!

I like to picture a circle on my right hip, and try to keep it at the same height during my downswing. Notice that when I do this, my knees remain stable and my belt line stays horizontal to the ground. If your right hip turns high like this, everything works.

WATCH & LEARN CREATE SOME HANDS-TO-EAR ROOM

As you take the clubhead away low, turn your shoulders while keeping your hands as far away from your right ear as possible [frame 1]. Once you're set, swing your right arm down so that you actually increase the distance between your right ear and your hands [frame 3]. Think of it as more of a downward move than a cast or a throw.
—**Dustin Johnson**

Scan this photo
to see D.J.'s swing in pure slow motion.

FINAL FIX

A Drill for Pure Contact

Hit drives from the sand to develop extra smash

If your swing fails to produce significant pop, it's likely you fall backward or to one side or the other in your finish, and you never really feel in control of the club or your swing. This is happening because you're not swinging with a consistent rhythm and balance. Elite drivers all have one thing in common: they have great balance.

Here's what you need to do: practice hitting your driver in the sand. Yes, it sounds unusual, but learning to swing with your feet in the sand is the perfect way to improve your balance and rhythm as well as your ballstriking.

To begin, find a practice bunker on the range with a relatively low lip and plenty of sand in the bottom. Tee a ball in the center of the hazard and take your address position with your driver, being sure your feet aren't dug down too deeply in the sand. Now make swings at about 60 percent of your normal speed, being sure to swing all the way to a complete finish.

After a while you should get comfortable hitting solid drives without losing your balance. Once you do, add more speed to your swing, but never so much that you lose control. When you're done, go to the grass part of the range and hit some drives while maintaining the same feel you had in the bunker. You should feel more powerful, rhythmic and balanced, and your drives should have more pop as well.

—*Top 100 Teacher*
Scott Sackett

Build better balance and rhythm by hitting drives from a bunker.

Scan this photo *to watch a video of this lesson.*

Hunter
Mahan

While there certainly are longer hitters, and many more who hit more fairways, very few golfers blend distance and accuracy in such efficient proportions as Hunter Mahan. With a ample amount of speed and the smarts to know when to swing for distance or control, Mahan has staked his claim as the Tour's ultimate driving machine.

Heavy on simplicity and light on difficult-to-time mechanics, Hunter Mahan's swing proves you can be accurate and long in equal amounts.

SKILL BREAKDOWN

Scan this photo *for a one-on-one lesson with Hunter Mahan.*

"The three modern swing elements that make up Hunter's technique are devoid of intricate moves and positions." —Brian Manzella

Pro File

Hunter Mahan

Full name Hunter Myles Mahan
Born May 17, 1982
Birthplace Orange, Calif.
Residence Colleyville, Texas
Height / Weight 5' 11" / 175 lbs.
College Oklahoma State University
Turned professional 2003
Professional victories 8 (5 PGA Tour)*
Majors None*
Career U.S. earnings $23.8 million*

*Through 2013 U.S. Open

With four Top 15s in the Total Driving statistic category in the last five years, Hunter Mahan thrives on finding position A off the tee. His swing is so free of idiosyncrasies that one could almost call it boring. But if boring means finding more fairways and knocking the ball 290 yards on an average day, we'll take it.

Mahan's swing is a compilation of popular and proven methods. In fact, if an archaeologist were to dig up Hunter's swing a thousand years from now, he'd probably note that it contained all of the en vogue techniques used in the early 21st century. Mahan doesn't move much off the ball when he turns; he swings on a flatter-than-normal plane and uses body turn instead of hand action to square the clubface at impact—three things taught on lesson tees by the majority of instructors every day.

So what does this mean for you? It means simplicity. The three modern swing elements that make up Hunter's technique are devoid of intricate moves and positions. **It's almost as though he turns back and through on a plane that's at a 90-degree angle to his spine, with his arms and hands simply coming along for the ride.** You've thrown a Frisbee before, right? Now, just imagine throwing it left-handed: You'd lead with your hips, turn like crazy and release the Frisbee with your hand at the very last moment. It's an easy way to create speed and accuracy.

—Top 100 Teacher Brian Manzella, English Turn Golf & C.C., New Orleans, La.

Rank File

PGA Tour Driving Distance/Accuracy

2007	296.7 yds/68.0%
2008	289.9 yds/66.0%
2009	297.0 yds/65.2%
2010	291.8 yds/68.0%
2011	291.6 yds/62.9%
2012	293.1 yds/67.7%

Stats courtesy of PGATour.com

SKILL PRACTICE

Keep Your Power Angle for Perfect Drives

The best drivers retain the bend in their right wrist deep into the downswing

By Top 100 Teacher MICHAEL BREED,
Manhattan Woods G.C., Pearl River, N.Y.

One of the reasons you're not driving the ball as well as you'd like is because you're not storing up enough potential power during your swing. This usually happens because you release the clubhead too early—a condition known as clubhead throwaway—which is causing you to lose your power angle.

To fix this problem you need to learn the sensation of storing your power angle (the angle between your forearm and clubshaft) late into your downswing. A great way to accomplish this is to perform my simple towel drill. Take an ordinary hand towel and wrap it around your driver shaft. Hold the grip as you normally would with your left hand and the ends of the towel with your right. Now make some swings, being sure to hold the towel tight enough to maintain the hinge in your left wrist and the angle between the clubshaft and your forearm as you swing the club down to the hitting zone each time (*photo, right*).

Everyone develops his or her own keys for learning this move, so pay close attention to the sensations you're feeling in your body while you perform the drill. Once you've made some swings with the towel, hit a few drives and try to re-create the same sensation you felt during the drill. You should quickly notice a more powerful feeling as you pass through impact.

Use a towel to get a feel for maintaining the power angle deep into your downswing. The secret angle to more power.

QUICK TIP
Open your mouth slightly and stick your tongue to the roof of your mouth. This relaxes the muscles in your face, jaw and neck, allowing you to make a faster, tension-free swing.

SKILL ANALYSIS

📷 **Scan this photo**
to see Mahan's swing
in pure slow motion.

*Classic address posture.
Amateurs should use more tilt and
a lower hand position.*

*A low-hands position at address
combined with zero arm roll sets
the clubhead outside the hands.*

*Elbows level with the ground—not a
bad position for amateurs to copy.*

*Upper body starting to "cover" the
ball at impact instead of backing up
and away (i.e., the amateur move).*

*Because he has cleared his lower
body, Mahan can extend his arms
through the ball at impact.*

*Both legs have snapped straight.
This is only effective if you can
maintain your posture like Mahan.*

WATCH & LEARN GET BORED WITH HITTING IT LONG AND STRAIGHT

Obviously, Hunter Mahan has built a swing without a lot of difficult-to-time parts, which is the main reason he's so accurate off the tee. So accurate it's almost boring to watch. All he has to do is rotate his hips faster or slower to dial in the distance required for the shot he's facing.

Notice in the sequence above how Mahan swings his hands straight back without rolling his forearms and wrists. This keeps the clubface pointed at the ball for a longer period of time during the backswing. Most amateurs tend to roll the club to the inside at the very start and whip the clubface too much open. This is the first bad move in a series that ultimately leads to slices. Mahan then uses his core and back muscles to wind all the way

to the top. Then, it's all on the feet, which he uses to grip the ground and call his legs into action at the start of his downswing. The trunk, arms and clubhead ultimately follow, whipping the club through the ball at max speed.

Despite what you've heard, Mahan proves that setup and impact are not the same. Compare frame 1 to frame 11 or the photo on page 36. At contact,

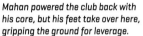

Mahan powered the club back with his core, but his feet take over here, gripping the ground for leverage.

Chest pointing well left of the target. A product of good technique and great flexibility.

Mahan is known for holding his finish longer than the average pro, probably because it's so good.

the hips and shoulders are open, the right arm is much more bent, the hands are higher than they are at address, his right heel is up—the list goes on and on. While you can't micromanage impact, painting the right picture in your mind can go a long way toward helping you master it time and again.
—*Top 100 Teacher Brady Riggs, Woodley Lakes G.C., Van Nuys, Calif.*

Try This! **The Straight-Drive Secret**

Make sure that your right shoulder is closer to the target than your left as you pass through impact. Think about your right hip, shoulder and lat all moving in a counterclockwise direction through impact and you'll have the correct feel. If you've done it right, a face-on view should show your right shoulder blocking the view of your left shoulder [*photo, right*], and your right pocket will be clearly visible.
—*Top 100 Teacher Chuck Winstead*

Scan this photo *to watch a video of this lesson.*

Yes!

Right shoulder closer to the target than the left.

STRAIGHT FROM THE SOURCE

Mahan on Mahan

"I've always been a decent driver, and one of the reasons why is that I really focus on my weight shift. A lot of amateurs make the mistake of shifting their weight immediately to their left heel at the start of the downswing. While it's a good sign that weight is actually moving left, putting it in your heel is a sure way to spin out of the shot and cut across the ball. I like to shift my weight into the toe of my left foot on my downswing, sort of diagonally across the ball. This allows me to get my energy moving forward yet rotate without pulling the club off plane."

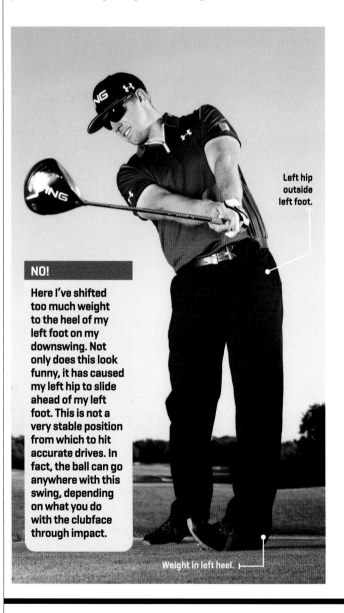

Left hip outside left foot.

NO!

Here I've shifted too much weight to the heel of my left foot on my downswing. Not only does this look funny, it has caused my left hip to slide ahead of my left foot. This is not a very stable position from which to hit accurate drives. In fact, the ball can go anywhere with this swing, depending on what you do with the clubface through impact.

Weight in left heel.

YES!

This position is ideal. Because I shifted my weight to the toe of my left foot at the start of the downswing, it's evenly distributed across the length of my left foot at impact and beyond. This allows me to make my normal turn, with my left hip directly over my left foot. This is a secret to accuracy not many people know about, but I've used it for a very long time with great success.

Left hip in line with left foot.

Weight across left foot.

STATS & SPECS

Mahan vs. the Field

Hunter Mahan has owned the Total Driving statistic category the last several seasons on Tour. The stat is computed by adding the player's rank in driving distance to the player's rank in driving accuracy.

2013 stats through Zurich Classic of New Orleans; courtesy of PGATour.com

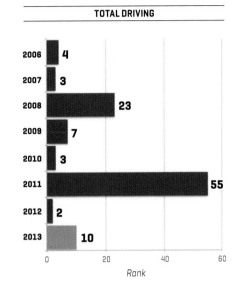

TOTAL DRIVING

Year	Rank
2006	4
2007	3
2008	23
2009	7
2010	3
2011	55
2012	2
2013	10

Rank

Mahan's Masher

PING G5
Loft 9.5 degrees
[*Set at 10.5 degrees*]
Shaft Aldilla Phenom NL 60
[*X flex, 45.25 inches*]
Swingweight D4
Tipping 0.5 inch

FINAL FIX

Use Your Eyes to Build a Better Driver Swing

Focusing with your left eye is the key to power

If you're like most amateurs, you fail to make a full turn in your backswing, which forces your arms and the club to pop up into the air. The reason you're doing this is because you're afraid to take your dominant (right) eye off the ball, and it's making you a poor driver. The key is to become accustomed to losing sight of the ball with your right eye and utilizing your left eye to see the ball at the top of your backswing. Once you develop this ability, you'll be able to make a much fuller backswing.

Step 1 Put an eye patch over your right eye or simply close your right eye.

Step 2 Hit 20 balls with your driver, keeping your right eye closed. Make a full turn away from the ball each time, making sure you keep your left eye focused on the ball.

Step 3 Take the patch off or open your right eye and try to replicate the same swing with a nice full turn. It shouldn't take you very long to feel comfortable using your left eye during your swing.

No!
Keeping your right eye on the ball restricts your turn.

Yes!

Look at the ball with your left eye for a better backswing.

As strange as it may sound, most Tour players hit more greens than they do fairways, which is a testament to elite players' ability to get on in regulation not only from good lies, but from every conceivable situation. Whether it's an approach from rough, sand or with the longest iron in your bag, Tour-proven iron-swing fundamentals will always get you home. To find out what these are we've assembled some of the greatest ballstrikers of this generation to show you the easy way to square up at impact and compress the ball on the clubface regardless of the situation you're in. If you copy their moves and follow the Top 100 Teachers' advice on how to blend them into your motion, the most difficult part of hitting the green will be deciding which club to pull.

To use the Scan-It/See-It feature in this section, look for the SCAN boxes [*example at right*]. For instructions, see page 9. Videos also available at golf.com/plap.

HOW TO PLAY LIKE...

- *Justin Rose*
  Get his ball control

- *Lee Westwood*
  Steal his long-iron swing

- *Sergio García*
  Get his ballstriking

- *Luke Donald*
  Copy his fairway
  bunker technique

- *Keegan Bradley*
  Get his versatility

Scan this photo
to access bonus
videos and lessons.

PLAY LIKE A PRO

SECTION 2
APPROACH
SHOTS

A thought-free swing
fueled by three main
swing triggers has made
Justin Rose one the most
accurate iron players on
the PGA Tour.

Justin
Rose

If there's one thing certain in golf, it's that 2013 U.S Open champion Justin Rose will hit the green if his drive lands in the fairway. With a newfound confidence in the swing he developed under the tutelage of coach Sean Foley, Rose has transformed what once was a statistical shortcoming—greens in regulation— into the most dominant part of his game. Nothing fancy, just proven swing fundamentals that never go out of style.

SKILL BREAKDOWN

Pro File

Justin Rose

Full name
Justin Peter Rose
Born July 30, 1980
Birthplace
Johannesburg,
South Africa
Residence
Orlando, Fla.
Height / Weight
6' 2" / 180 lbs.
College None
Turned professional
1998
Professional victories
16 (5 PGA Tour)*
Majors 2013 U.S.
Open*
Career U.S. earnings
$24.1 million*

*Through 2013 U.S. Open

"Triggers exist throughout his motion and allow Justin to ignore mechanics and put his swing on autopilot."—Mike Adams

At the 2010 Players Championship Justin Rose hit four flagsticks in a row on the practice range, then promptly went out and shot 72–72 and missed the cut. That made the Brit 0-for-152 in tournaments on American soil at the time. Then, he won two of the next four events he entered. Credit goes to his coach, Sean Foley. Since working with Sean, Rose has gone from 70th in the Official World Golf Ranking to a solid position in the Top 10.

Everyone knows Foley as a technician, but he's pragmatic, too, and worked with Rose to replace hard-set positions with feels and triggers. These triggers exist throughout his motion and allow Justin to ignore mechanics and put his swing on autopilot. He starts by moving the clubhead first—a great feeling to establish good tempo. He triggers his downswing by pulling his left arm across his chest. **What's your trigger? If you're a slicer, it's probably to spin your shoulders, a death move that creates an outside-in swing.** Rose then gets the club to wrap around the back of his neck. Keeping this vision in mind is a great way to keep from hanging back and flipping the clubhead at the ball instead of driving through it.

These are easy triggers that pull the whole swing together, and Rose is using them all to become the most consistent iron player on Tour.
—*Top 100 Teacher Mike Adams, The Medalist Club, Hobe Sound, Fla., and Hamilton Farm G.C., Gladstone, N.J.*

Rank File

PGA Tour Greens in Regulation

From > 200 yds.
56.8%

From 175–200 yds.
59.7%

From 150–175 yds.
68.0%

From 125–150 yds.
79.6%

From < 125 yds.
82.8%

Stats from 2012 season; courtesy of PGATour.com

SKILL PRACTICE

Set up.   Extend your left arm.   Turn and "go get it!"

Scan this photo to watch a video of this lesson.

How to Strike Your Irons Square and Pure

My "go get it" drill teaches you how to turn through the ball like a Tour pro

By Top 100 Teacher MIKE PERPICH, RiverPines G.C., Johns Creek, Ga.

Most amateurs fail to get all the way through the ball, which explains why they rarely compress it or generate that nice "click" sound at impact. (You're used to hearing more of a "thud.") Golfers with this problem typically have decent backswings and downswings but tend to hold back through impact, choosing to swing their arms through the hitting zone instead of busting through it with their body. Get the correct feel—and better compression—with the following drill:

Step 1 Set up with any one of your mid-irons, using your regular stance and address posture. You won't need to hit a ball with this drill.

Step 2 Without moving anything else, extend your left arm and club down the target line. You want your shaft and forearm as close to horizontal as possible, with the toe of the club pointing up.

Step 3 While keeping your left arm and club in place, reach for the grip and reset your right hand on the handle. I tell my students, "Go get it!" Notice how you instinctively shift your weight and turn your lower body to get your right hand on the club again. You can't do it just by swinging your right arm (the move you make when you hit bad shots on the course). Practice this drill a few times to ingrain the feel of correctly turning through the ball, then hit a few shots for real.

SKILL ANALYSIS

Athletic address—bent from the hips with the back flat.

The clubhead has moved a few feet but the hips have rotated just a few degrees. Patience.

Upper left arm pressed against the chest—a key pressure point.

Left arm perfectly in line with the shaft.

Hips slowing, arms accelerating. It's the perfect sequence for a perfect impact.

Upper body still tilted sideways toward the ball.

Left arm, left wrist and clubface aligned just as they were at the address position.

WATCH & LEARN THREE KEYS FOR A SOLID IRON SWING

The son of a golf professional, Justin Rose has long seen great value in coaching. His teachers have included Ken Rose (his late father), instruction legend David Leadbetter, Nick Bradley and Sean Foley. Working with Foley since 2009, Justin has developed a motion that closely resembles the stack-and-tilt method of Mike Bennett and Andy Plummer. In his backswing, Justin

neatly pivots around his spine while keeping his shoulders pretty much centered over the ball. Coming down, he aggressively shifts his weight toward his left side and slides his hips to the left more than you normally see, even with Tour players. That's because Justin's goal is to get all his weight onto—and all his force against—his left leg, the hallmark trait of the stack-and-tilt.

Rose's extremely steep downswing path and big lateral weight shift are excellent for hitting irons (which demand a very descending blow). Still, Justin, now 33, is playing the best golf of his 16-year career because he's finally gaining intimate trust and confidence in his technique.

During your takeaway, copy Justin and keep forearm rotation to a

As his hips and shoulders unwind, his weight shifts aggressively to the left side.

From start to finish, Rose never loses his tilt toward the contact point.

Pro Take Justin Rose's Go-to Move

"As soon as I contact the ball I'm thinking 'low exit.' I want my right arm and shaft to swing to the left of the target on roughly the same plane as my left shoulder. This type of shallow exit allows your body turn to keep pace with the speed of the clubhead.

The secret is to keep your left biceps in tight to your body in the follow-through and allow your left elbow to 'roll' against your torso. It won't actually stay pinned, because of the rotational force of your swing, but it's a great trigger to keep your swing tight and your arms from disconnecting from your body. When you feel the clubhead moving low and left after impact, you're starting to get the right feel."
—**Justin Rose**

No! Left arm off chest.

Yes! Left arm connected to chest.

Try This! | Stabilize Your Swing for Better Compression

minimum. Then, keep your left arm fully extended and tight against your chest as you move the club to the top. Coming down, make sure the clubface is square to the path (the arc the clubhead is traveling on) all the way to impact. Practice these moves in slow motion at first to make sure you have them nailed, then slowly add speed.
—*Top 100 Teacher Brady Riggs*

To strike your irons with authority you need to stop moving around during your swing. Take an empty ball bucket and place it between your feet in your normal address position as shown. Hit some shots while maintaining contact with both the ground and the bucket throughout your full motion. This should eliminate any excess lower-body action in your swing and greatly improve your contact.
—**Top 100 Teacher Mark Hackett**

STRAIGHT FROM THE SOURCE

Rose on Rose

"You're pretty adept at striking your irons solidly, but you don't always hit your target. One possible reason is that your alignment at address is faulty. If you unwittingly align to the left or right of your target, your body will react by rerouting the club in the middle of your swing. You can't play consistent golf this way. I always use the same simple method to line up my iron shots, and it continues to work for me. Here's how to do it."

Step 1 Get behind the ball and pick a very specific target. Don't just aim at the green—select a tree behind the green, a shadow on the putting surface or something else specific. I like to aim with my club as though I'm plumb-bobbing a putt. It helps me lock in on the target. Line up your target like you do when you plumb-bob a putt.

Point the face at an intermediate target

Give your real target a final look.

Look back at the ball and immediately start your swing.

Step 2 Pick an intermediate target about three or four feet in front of your ball, like a leaf or a blade of grass. It's much easier to aim at a close target than at something that's 150 yards away. Once you have your intermediate target, make sure the clubface is aimed directly at it.

Step 3 Step into your stance without altering your clubface angle. Make sure that you have your intermediate target lined up and then take one good look at your chosen target.

Step 4 Don't spend too much time thinking about the shot or the results. Once you're comfortable and balanced in your setup, look back at the ball and fire away. Trust your aim and confidently start the club back.

STATS & SPECS

Rose vs. the Field

Justin Rose led the PGA Tour in Greens in Regulation in 2012 and was the only player to crack the 70 percent threshold that season. And he's not just good from the middle of the fairway. Justin was nearly 10 percentage points better at hitting the green from places other than the short grass. Good technique pays off anywhere.

Stats from 2012 season; courtesy of PGATour.com

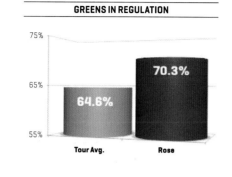

GREENS IN REGULATION

75%

65%

55%

64.6% — Tour Avg.

70.3% — Rose

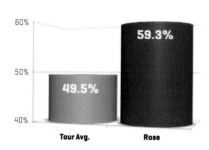

GREENS HIT FROM OTHER THAN THE FAIRWAY

60%

50%

40%

49.5% — Tour Avg.

59.3% — Rose

Specialty Gear

Hit It Better with Your Feet

I've been wearing soft shoes for a few seasons now (*photo, below*). I'm a big believer in them. I do all of my gym work with a barefoot mentality, meaning I don't wear ultra-stabilizing footwear when I work out. Adding stability kind of turns off your circuits and core muscles, while taking a bit of it away forces you to work more efficiently. These shoes do exactly that, plus they're more comfortable than the classic-style shoes I used to wear. I never feel tired after a round.—*Justin Rose*

QUICK TIP
Make sure your eyes are still in line with the shaft in your follow-though. If you do it correctly, your spine will be bent to the right, which keeps the club moving correctly through the hitting zone.

FINAL FIX

Make a Natural Backswing for Better Contact

A simple trick to set the club on plane

Scan this photo *to watch a video of this lesson.*

To find the right kind of backswing for you, get some quick help from a friend and perform the following test.

Step 1 Swing to your mid-backswing position and have your friend lay an alignment stick or club along your shoulder line. You want the club you're swinging and the alignment stick to be parallel to one another.

Step 2 Move the club until it matches the alignment stick, regardless of where

that is. Once you find the spot, hold it for a few seconds until you can memorize its exact location.

Step 3 Hit this spot in your backswing consistently and you'll start swinging more from the inside on your downswing. Your angle of attack will be shallower, too, and your ballstriking and control will improve dramatically. Plus, it'll make it very difficult for you to produce a slice.

—*Top 100 Teacher Mike Adams*

No! A mismatch in shaft angle and shoulder line leads to poor contact.

Yes! Matching the shaft angle to the shoulder line means you're on plane.

Skill No. 6
LONG IRONS

Lee
Westwood

Armed with perfect timing and natural strength, Lee Westwood can attack pins from any yardage and is especially dangerous from long-iron range. His innate talent aside, Westwood proves that grasping the skills required for short swings pays dividends with your 3-, 4- and 5-irons as well.

Strength and a near-perfect delivery position help Lee Westwood get close to the pin from distances where other players are happy just to get on.

SKILL BREAKDOWN

"As kind of a working-class golf hero, Westwood's plodding style suggests that he's more concerned with the processes of improvement than the rewards that follow." —Jon Tattersall

As kind of a working-class golf hero, Westwood's plodding style suggests that he's more concerned with the processes of improvement than the rewards that follow. And while his swing isn't pretty by today's Tour standards, Westwood has a few, key dynamic moves you can use, especially when you reach those uncomfortable distances beyond 185 yards.

Setup With a long iron, position the ball just forward of center and take a slightly wider stance for extra balance.

Backswing Set the appropriate long-iron swing pace by making a smooth backswing and tracing a wide arc. Patience here allows you to make a smoother transition and a better downswing sequence without feeling rushed.

Downswing If you fall over when you hit your long irons, it's probably because you're hanging back too much in an effort to help the ball into the air. Swing all the way through the shot until your belt buckle is facing the target in the finish and you'll get much better results. **Also, try this: Hit the ball hard. Like Lee, take a mighty lash!** You won't hit every shot perfectly, but this aggressive mind-set simplifies things and, honestly, is a lot more fun.

—*Top 100 Teacher Jon Tattersall, Terminus Club, Atlanta, Ga.*

SKILL PRACTICE

Scan this photo *to watch a video of this lesson.*

RIGHT KNEE
Flex it toward the target, not away from your body.

RIGHT ANKLE
Roll it gently toward the target in unison with your right knee.

RIGHT HIP
Rotate it toward the target, not out toward the target line.

Release the Club with Your Body for Better Ballstriking

Let your right hip, knee and ankle move toward the target for squarer hits with longer clubs

**By Top 100 Teacher RICK McCORD,
Orange Lake C.C., Orlando, Fla.**

Your long-iron game is inconsistent, not very accurate and not very long. Good players know that the key to swinging with consistency and making solid contact with not only the long irons but with every iron in the bag is to control the club with the body rather than the arms and hands. Even if you have an extremely strong upper body, you'll get significantly better leverage, speed and control if you use your lower half to power the club. The three areas of your body you need to focus on to do it properly are your right hip, right knee and right ankle. Get these working properly and you'll be releasing with your body in no time.

The key is to get all three elements working toward the target—not away from it—as you swing the club down from the top. Practice by swinging slowly and making sure your right knee folds gently toward your left as you deliver the club to the impact zone. At the same time, flex your right ankle toward the target while rotating your right hip so it, too, is moving toward the target. In instruction circles, this is known as a right-side release, and it's the secret to more power and greater accuracy.

QUICK TIP
Keep your head centered over the impact area. This allows you to make your swing as wide as possible on the target side of the ball (just as you should on your backswing).

SKILL ANALYSIS

WATCH & LEARN HOW TO KNOCK IT STIFF FROM LONG RANGE

Lee Westwood is Europe's most consistent player thanks to his mastery of the most important elements of the swing: a square clubface and an on-line path. Lee's isn't a one-plane swing, a stack-and-tilt move or any other method—it's just a swing that features the old-fashioned fundamentals that make good players great. His lone quirk is that he drops his head several inches from the start of his swing to impact. While this isn't ideal, it doesn't affect his clubface position or swing path. If you're looking for consistency in your game, Westwood is your go-to role model.
—*Top 100 Teacher Brady Riggs*

BACKSWING

Lee's improved fitness allows him to limit his hip rotation but still create enough turn with his upper body. The clubface is dead square (the leading edge is perpendicular to the ground and parallel to the outside of his left arm).

DOWNSWING

Take note of his hand, arm and club position—they're perfect! So perfect you should carry this picture in your wallet for constant reference. The clubshaft is pointing parallel to his toes, his right elbow is tight to his right hip, and he has maintained his spine angle perfectly.

IMPACT

Westwood isn't making a massive hip turn through the ball, but he still has the look of an athlete. His straight legs indicates that he's "jumping" away from the ground. His excessive head dive produces a very steep shoulder angle and a slight "chicken-wing" in his right arm.

STATS & SPECS

Westwood vs. the Field

The chart at right proves just how deadly Lee Westwood is with a long-iron in his hands, even when compared with the best players in the world. From 200 to 225 yards (probably a 4-iron for Lee) he lands the ball about 18 percent closer to the pin than his peers. From 225 to 250 yards (a 3-iron), he's 20 percent more accurate.

Stats from 2012 season; courtesy of PGATour.com

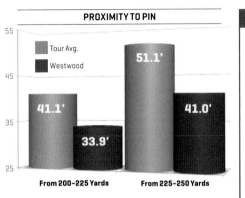

PROXIMITY TO PIN

- Tour Avg.
- Westwood

Feet

From 200–225 Yards: 41.1' (Tour Avg.), 33.9' (Westwood)
From 225–250 Yards: 51.1' (Tour Avg.), 41.0' (Westwood)

Westwood's Weapons

PING i20 (3–PW)
D1 swingweight
Shaft PING JZ steel with Cushin (*S Flex, + .25 inch*)
Grip PING ID8 half-cord (*white*)

FINISH

Westwood never stops turning, which is why he gets away with his bent left arm position at impact. Regardless of the club you're swinging, the goal is to get your right shoulder closer to the target than your left at the finish.

FINAL FIX

Use Lag with Long Irons

Do what all great players do—strike the ball first

If iron deficiency is killing your scores, it's probably because you fail to keep the angle between your left forearm and the clubshaft deep enough into your downswing ("clubhead lag"). Instead, you throw the club from the top, causing it to bottom out too early and hit the ground first and the ball second. It's supposed to be the other way around.

You form the angle when you hinge your wrists on your backswing. Some players create it early in the backswing, while others wait until the club is nearly at the top. Regardless, all good players produce it and, more importantly, retain it deep into the downswing. The audible *click* you hear when a good player strikes the ball is the result of the shaft leaning forward at impact and the clubhead driving down and through.

To learn how to retain your lag and create ball-first contact like an elite iron player, practice making slow-motion swings following these steps.

Step 1 As you swing down from the top, fight the urge to push the clubhead down with your right wrist. You know you're doing it correctly if the shaft and clubhead are still behind your hands when your left hand is under your left shoulder (*photo, above right*).

Step 2 Now, drive your left hip to the left so that your arms, hands and club are driven down through the hitting zone. Let your left wrist bow away from the target. This will keep your hands in front of the ball at impact—the secret to crisp, pro-like contact (*photo, below right*).
—**Top 100 Teacher Chuck Evans**

BALLSTRIKING

Sergio Garcia

When your hands lead the club on the downswing, it's called lag, and nobody lags better than Sergio. Most elite golfers produce 90 degrees of lag, but García creates in excess of 100 with a move so volatile that he's trying to tone it down. Regardless, it's the main move among many that has made Sergio García one of the greatest ballstrikers of his generation.

There are ballstrikers and then there are ballstriking legends. Sergio García is the latter, with a lag-heavy downswing that's second to none.

SKILL BREAKDOWN

Scan this photo *for a one-on-one lesson with Sergio.*

"Any good golfer can create lag, but nobody—*nobody*—knows how to release it like García."—Brian Manzella

Pro File

Sergio García

Full name Sergio García Fernández
Nickname El Niño
Born January 9, 1980
Birthplace Castellón, Spain
Residence Borriol, Spain
Height / Weight 5' 10" / 160 lbs.
College None
Turned professional 1999
Professional victories 24 (8 PGA Tour)*
Majors None*
Career U.S. earnings $31.9 million*

*Through 2013 U.S. Open

Sergio García's iron swing is in the Top 10—maybe Top 5—of all time. At the very least, it's the best low-plane swing of the past 40 years. With moves like Sergio's, you can't help but hit your irons perfect.

While many point to Sergio's tremendous clubhead lag as his key swing trait, most of these folks are missing the point. Any good golfer can create lag, but nobody—*nobody*—knows how to release it like García. Most lag guys drag the handle through impact. Sergio lets it all go. The man doesn't get enough credit for how dynamic—or good—his swing really is.

I've looked at García's swing from every angle and at every speed, and while he's definitely one of the best at using a pulling motion from the top to create lag, he never really pulls straight toward the ground. Sergio's hands go down, but they also go out toward the target line. They also move to his right. In fact, nobody's hands move away from the target from the top as much as Sergio's. If he really were pulling a chain, as he says he does on page 64, it would be on more of a 45-degree angle.

My advice: Drop your hands as Sergio advises, but **experiment with moving your hands away from your right ear and out toward the target line.** This will help you keep your back pointed at the target longer, which is always a benefit.

—*Top 100 Teacher Brian Manzella, English Turn Golf & C.C., New Orleans, La.*

Rank File

PGA Tour
Proximity to Pin

From 75–100 yards
13' 11"

From 100–125 yards
18' 5"

From 125–150 yards
24' 10"

From 150–175 yards
26' 5"

From 175–200 yards
31' 8"

Stats from 2012 season; courtesy of PGATour.com

SKILL PRACTICE

Scan this photo to watch a video of this lesson.

No!

Instep up, bottle down.

Yes!

Instep down, bottle up.

Maintaining contact with the ground will help you strike your irons solidly.

Use Your Feet to Catch Irons Crisply

A bottle can show you how to improve your impact with better footwork

By Top 100 Teacher KEITH LYFORD, Old Greenwood G.C., Truckee, Calif.

Your footwork is sloppy and it's having a negative effect on your iron play. Your big mistake is allowing your right heel to come off the ground and rotate counterclockwise around your toe during the downswing. This causes your right knee to shoot toward the target way too early, destroying your swing path. To create solid compression on your iron shots, you need to do a better job of staying connected to the ground.

To make sure you keep your right heel and instep connected to the ground properly during your iron swing, try this simple drill: Take a water, soda or beer bottle and place it behind your right foot as you settle into your address position. Your goal is to be able to hit solid iron shots while keeping your foot planted firmly on the ground. If you do it correctly, you should be able to hit shots without touching or knocking over the bottle. If you knock it over well after the ball has been hit, that's okay. However, it's best to be able to hit shot after shot with the bottle still standing. If you knock the bottle over on every swing, try leaning your right heel toward the target on your downswing instead of allowing it to spin out.

QUICK TIP
Have a friend hold an iron shaft so that it's parallel to your sight line when you look down at the ball. Practice making swings so that at the finish your eyes are still in line with the shaft.

SKILL ANALYSIS

Scan this photo to see García's swing in pure slow motion.

Tall, "proud" posture with high hands at address.

Shaft parallel to toe (and target) line, and elbows the same distance from each other as at address.

Left arm straight and left hand "pushing" the club away from his body.

Perfect: The shaft is loaded and ready to release underneath the right forearm.

Power comes when the hands slow down and the clubhead picks up speed.

Still over the shot, with eyes looking at the contact point.

WATCH & LEARN MAKE A DOWNSWING PLANE SWITCH

Sergio García's full swing, developed under the tutelage of his father, has featured the same shape since he burst onto the scene as a teenager. I first saw Sergio in the late 1990s, when he was an amateur playing a round with Mark O'Meara at Isleworth. His action was as impressive that afternoon as it is today—García's swing is still one of the most dynamic and explosive out there.

Many of the swing traits that separate Sergio from the rest might be difficult for an amateur to copy, but they still warrant discussion—you should at least become aware of the way power and speed develop in their purest forms.

First, notice how he drops from the shoulder plane almost immediately to the shaft plane at the start of his downswing. **This is the definition of lag,** **and the only way to get it—and supersize your power—is to flatten your approach, as Sergio does.** You can see how fast he is by the fact that his hands barely move through impact, yet the clubhead speeds through the ball and down the target line. The club responds to the lag by releasing swiftly and naturally. Important point. You don't "do" a release, it simply happens.

Flattening the shaft angle to set up his signature lag power.

The sharpest power angle (formed between the left arm and clubshaft) in the game.

He's maintained a consistent angle and distance between his elbows from start to finish.

Spine still tilted toward the impact point. Perfect.

Try This! Pull the Club Up

1 Making your downswing plane flatter than your backswing plane is the secret to creating lag.
2 Trust your release—let the clubhead go after impact without steering it.
3 Maintain your posture. Try squatting a bit in the downswing—it helps.
—*Top 100 Teacher Mitchell Spearman, Isleworth Golf & C.C., Windermere, Fla., and Doral Arrowwood, Rye Brook, N.Y.*

Feel like you're trying to yank the shaft out of the clubhead in order to swing faster through impact. That means pulling the grip and shaft up—not pushing across—as you power through the ball. Pull the handle toward your stomach as soon as the clubhead gets below your hands in your downswing and keep pulling until after impact. You'll feel a faster swing as the clubhead reacts to the pulling action by accelerating down and through the ball.—*Top 100 Teacher Brian Manzella*

Scan this photo
to watch a video of this lesson.

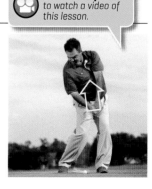

STRAIGHT FROM THE SOURCE

Sergio on Sergio

"In my opinion, the two worst things you can do for your swing are (1) spin your shoulders too early from the top of your backswing (*photo, below*), and (2) lose the angle between your left forearm and the clubshaft before you come into the ball. The first error will lead to nothing but a heavy dose of slices and pulls. Losing your lag—the second error—will quickly make you the shortest hitter in your foursome."

DON'T DO THIS

The worst error you can make: spinning your shoulders open too early from the top.

No!

MY MAIN MOVE

Once I'm at the top, I think about keeping my right shoulder behind me until I'm done transitioning from from my backswing to my downswing. When I'm swinging at my best, my shoulders are the last thing to move as I make my way back down toward the ball.

STATS & SPECS

Sergio in the Rankings

Since bursting onto the scene and battling Tiger Woods to the very end at the 1999 PGA Championship as a 19-year-old, Sergio García has held several lofty spots in the official world golf rankings, including the No. 2 rung in 2002. For the past 15 years, El Niño has averaged 16th, thanks to driving power and one of the best iron swings in golf.

16.5

García's average end-of-year rank since 1999.

QUICK TIP

As you swing past impact, allow your left arm to continue to rotate so that the knuckles on your left hand turn toward the ground in your follow-through.

Garcia's Gear

TaylorMade RocketBladez Tour
Clubs 3–PW
Lie 1 degree flat
Length -0.5 inch
Shaft Nippon N.S. Pro Tour 130 [*X flex*]

FINAL FIX

How to Hit the Sweet Spot

An extra club gives you better balance in a single swing

There are multiple causes of off-center hits, but the most common is poor balance. The long-term fix is to establish better balance when you swing. Hefty task. In the meantime, try the following quick fixes:

Scan this photo *to watch a video of this lesson.*

IF YOU TEND TO CATCH SHOTS ON THE HEEL...
...hit balls with a club placed under your toes. This will force you to keep your weight on your heels instead of moving forward.

IF YOU TEND TO CATCH SHOTS ON THE TOE...
...hit balls with a club placed under your heels. This will force you to keep your weight forward when you swing so you don't fall backward.

IF YOU TEND TO MAKE CONTACT ALL OVER THE CLUBFACE...
...hit balls with a club placed under the balls of your feet. This will center your weight so you don't fall back or forward when you swing.

—Top 100 Teacher Rod Lidenberg

Luke
Donald

British star Luke Donald has always been known as a master of greenside sand play, but he's similarly adept at getting on the green from fairway bunkers. Like most pros, Donald finds fairway sand only about once a round, but it's never cause for a lost stroke, thanks to a rock-solid technique that consistently ensures ball-first contact and guards against taking too much sand.

Luke Donald doesn't do anything special in a fairway bunker other than apply the same full-swing techniques that made him one of the best iron players of all time.

SKILL BREAKDOWN

"You'll get better—more Luke-like—results if you use an extra club and swing easy." —Eden Foster

One of the reasons why former world No. 1 Luke Donald is so good at hitting greens in regulation from fairway bunkers is that his iron technique is so solid. In fact, as he has risen to become of the best iron players in the game, his GIR percentage from fairway bunkers has skyrocketed (*see stats, right*). When the ball is in the fairway, the goal is to contact the ball first and then the ground. **The same method applies to fairway bunkers, where you want to keep club/sand interaction to a minimum.** (This is the opposite of what you want to do in a greenside bunker, where you actually want to contact only the sand.)

In this section you'll learn several ways to escape fairway bunkers with ease and increase your chances of hitting the green. My advice is to use the same techniques as when swinging an iron from the fairway, but with a few adjustments to ensure ball-first, not sand-first, contact.

The first alteration is to choke down on the grip slightly. Then, take a wider stance and try to keep your lower body still. You want to feel flat-footed, so you won't overuse your legs. As you settle into your address, check that the ball is slightly back of center. This is another easy trick to ensure you contact the ball before any sand.

When you go to make your swing, keep your lower body quiet. In fact, your feet shouldn't move at all from where they were at address. Doing so allows you to strike a solid blow while helping you avoid the common fairway-bunker mistake of trying to hit the ball too hard. You'll get better—more Luke-like—results if you use an extra club and swing easy.

—*Top 100 Teacher Eden Foster, Maidstone Club, East Hampton, N.Y.*

Rank File

PGA Tour GIR from Fairway Bunker

Year	%	Rank
2009	37.5%	[144th]
2010	43.8%	[136th]
2011	61.0%	[5th]
2012	59.5%	[8th]

Stats courtesy of PGATour.com

SKILL PRACTICE

Scan this photo *to watch a video of this lesson.*

Catching the ball a little thin in a fairway bunker will help you get the full distance from your club and fly the ball all the way to the green.

QUICK TIP
You don't always have to use an iron in a fairway bunker. Grab your hybrid and make an easier swing. The ball will easily clear the front lip and land close—if not on—the green.

Fly It All the Way from a Fairway Bunker

When you're stuck on the beach, thin it to win it

By Top 100 Teacher TOM STICKNEY, *Bighorn G.C., Palm Desert, Calif., and Promontory G.C., Park City, Utah*

Like most amateurs, you treat a shot from a fairway bunker like any other sand shot and take too much sand at impact, causing the ball to come up way short of the green. The key to getting the full distance out of any club from a fairway bunker is to make contact with the ball first and then the sand. (In greenside bunkers you only want to make contact with the sand.) It's also what you need from a clean lie in the fairway, but since most amateurs aren't very good at taking a divot after the ball on a regular shot (i.e., hit the ball first and the ground second), you need to take special care when in a fairway bunker.

To improve your performance from sand, try the following drill, which should help you get a feel for "thinning" your sand shots.

At the Range Tee up a practice ball just barely above the turf, with the stripe on the ball set parallel to the ground. Your goal is to simply catch the stripe with the leading edge of your iron. That should give you the right kind of contact to carry the shot the full distance, while avoiding most of the sand behind the ball.

On the Course When you face this shot for real during your round, picture the stripe on the equator of the ball (like the one on the practice ball) and make that your contact point. You'll fly it all the way to the green out of the sand every time.

SKILL ANALYSIS

WATCH & LEARN
PUNCH IT OUT FROM FAIRWAY SAND

If you're so vexed by fairway sand that you don't think about hitting the green, or tend to hit behind the ball on the times that you do, opt for a punch shot that lands short of the green and works its way on. You'll see a lot of Tour pros do this from time to time, especially from the common 150-yard range. Follow the cues on this page.
—*Top 100 Teacher Rod Lidenberg, Prestwick G.C., Woodbury, Minn.*

SWING

Start your swing by hinging your wrists quickly back in a narrow arc. Cut your backswing when your hands reach hip height—that's all the power you'll need.

CLUB

Choose a 6-, 7- or 8-iron, depending on your distance to the pin. With a 6-iron, a bunker punch will give you 100 yards of carry and 50 yards of roll. The ball will fly low and run out onto the green.

IMPACT

From the top, pinch your knees and focus on making ball-first contact. Keep your wrists firm at impact—you don't want to lose the clubshaft angle you created at address. Since all you're looking to do is to punch the ball, your finish is of little consequence.

ADDRESS

Set up with the ball back of center and the shaft leaning forward. Align the clubface square to the target. Take a narrow stance with more of your weight on your left foot and your sternum in front of the ball to create a downward angle of attack.

STATS & SPECS

Donald vs. the Field

Recent stats show Luke Donald excels at reaching the green from a fairway bunker compared with even the best players in the world. The numbers also prove that finding sand off the tee doesn't have to result in a bogey—or worse. In 2012, Donald scored 13 percent lower than the Tour average on holes where the tee shot landed in fairway sand.

Stats from 2012 season; courtesy of PGATour.com

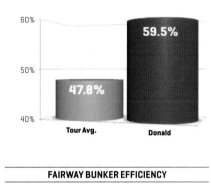

GIR FROM FAIRWAY BUNKER

- Tour Avg. — 47.8%
- Donald — 59.5%

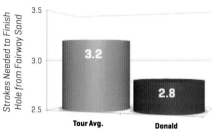

FAIRWAY BUNKER EFFICIENCY

Strokes Needed to Finish Hole from Fairway Sand

- Tour Avg. — 3.2
- Donald — 2.8

Luke's Irons

Mizuno MP-64
Shaft True Temper Dynamic Gold S300 [*S flex*]
Loft/Lie Standard

FINAL FIX

"Reach" in a Fairway Bunker

This setup trick gives you a clean escape every time

You automatically lose at least one extra stroke every time your ball lands in a fairway bunker. That's because you don't have a reliable and consistent technique for these shots, and you typically dig your club too deep into the sand and fail to get the ball back to the fairway, let alone all the way to your intended target.

The simple way to beat these tough lies is to set up with the ball off the toe of the club. This ball position will force you to reach out to make contact and will naturally flatten your swing a bit and add loft at impact. The result will be more ball-first contact with less sand, and shots that get out of the bunker quickly and actually fly relatively far due to the lack of spin you'll create at impact. Try it—I guarantee that your fairway bunker woes will be over for good.

—*Top 100 Teacher Ron Gring, Magnolia Grove G.C., Mobile, Ala.*

Scan this photo to watch a video of this lesson.

To reduce the amount of sand you take at impact, play the ball off the toe...

...instead of in the center.

Keegan **Bradley**

With one of the best rookie seasons in recent memory under his belt [the 2011 campaign, which ended with his victory at the PGA Championship], Keegan Bradley continues to shine not only as one of the great power hitters of his generation, but a versatile iron player who can hit the green from almost every lie imaginable.

Hitting the green regardless of the circumstances is usually the calling card of a cagey veteran, not a third-year player like Keegan Bradley.

SKILL BREAKDOWN

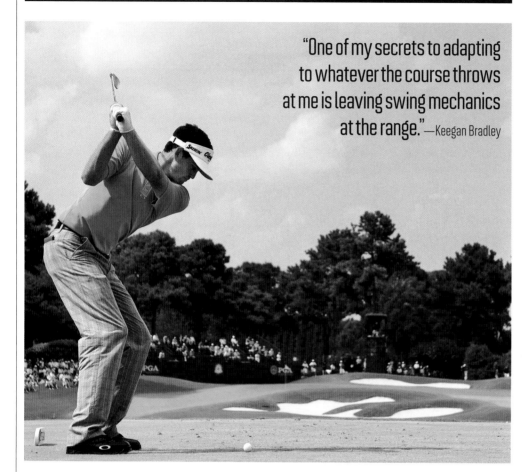

"One of my secrets to adapting to whatever the course throws at me is leaving swing mechanics at the range." —Keegan Bradley

Pro File

Keegan Bradley

Full name Keegan Hansen Bradley
Nickname Keegs
Born June 7, 1986
Birthplace Woodstock, Vt.
Residence Jupiter, Fla.
Height / Weight 6' 3" / 190 lbs.
College St. John's University
Turned professional 2008
Professional victories 7 [3 PGA Tour]*
Majors 2012 PGA Championship*
Career U.S. earnings $9.8 million *

*Through 2013 U.S. Open

Rank File

PGA Tour All-Around Rank

Year	Rank
2011	34th
2012	1st
2013	13th*

*Through U.S. Open

Stats courtesy of PGATour.com

My win at the 2011 PGA Championship was clutch—I played my best golf when it mattered most. Even though it was the first major I ever entered, and I have yet to log 70 events on the PGA Tour, I've been prepping to play at the highest level for a very long time. My aunt, LPGA Hall-of-Famer Pat Bradley, told me long ago that the secret to golf success is finding how to get the most from your swing—even when it's off—on every shot you face, especially when you're in a less-than-perfect situation.

One of my secrets to adapting to whatever the course throws at me is leaving swing mechanics at the range. When you're on the course, you have to go with the swing that the day gives you. And since you can't always control what your swing is doing, it's crucial that you learn how to control what happens before it. I walk to the ball thinking of nothing but where I want it to go. **You can almost will the ball where you want it to go if you focus on your target long enough.** This is encouraging on the days your swing isn't doing what it's supposed to. Here's how I do it:

1 Pick a landing spot, and make it precise. Don't say "the middle of the green." Say "that small patch of dark grass in the middle of the green."

2 Stare at your target—and I mean stare—as you settle into your stance. Lock it in to your brain, and stay focused on it.

3 Don't rush your swing. If you're not feeling 100 percent committed, stand back. Relax and repeat steps 1 and 2. If you're still not comfortable, make your target a little bigger.
—Keegan Bradley

SKILL PRACTICE

Reach Any Green from the Rough

The secret: low hands from start to finish

Scan this photo to watch a video of this lesson.

1 Hands low.

2 Weight on your front side.

3 Steep swing.

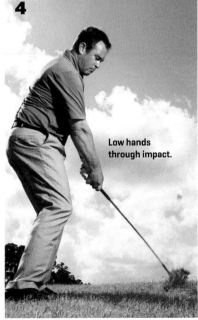

4 Low hands through impact.

By Top 100 Teacher **MARK HACKETT,** *Old Palm G.C., Palm Beach Gardens, Fla.*

You're not always going to split the fairway with your drive, and part of keeping your scores from ballooning is knowing how to get on the green in regulation from challenging lies. The most common bad lie is rough. If you have difficulty advancing the ball from tall grass, you may be swinging too much around your body. While this type of swing is good for hitting power draws off the tee, it doesn't work in tall grass, where you need steepness to catch the ball cleanly and get it airborne.

Escaping the thick stuff is easy, but only if you know how to alter your setup and swing to produce the necessary steepness. Follow these steps:

Step 1 Stand farther from the ball with your hands low. This will cause your shoulders to tilt, setting up a steeper swing path. You should feel that your chest is more on top of the ball.

Step 2 Set your weight over your forward leg. Position the ball in the middle or even a bit back in your stance, with your hands set in front of your belt buckle.

Step 3 Fight the urge to hit down on the ball, up on the ball or to otherwise help it into the air. Simply swing the club with good pace. Your address position and forward weight distribution automatically set you up for success.

Step 4 As you swing through impact, keep your hands low, just as they were at address. This will give you the maximum amount of leverage to power the club through the rough.

SKILL ANALYSIS

WATCH & LEARN SWING ON CORRECT TRACK

Keegan Bradley is a perfect example of a mid-track golfer. Because of the way he's built, his ideal clubhead path is defined by the plane that extends from the target line through the tip of his right elbow at address (right-arm plane). **Bradley makes his best swings when he takes the club back and delivers the club to the ball along his right-arm plane.**

If you're a mid-track (right-arm-plane) golfer like Bradley, you should feel as though you're delivering the club to the ball using only your trunk (hips to chest). Think about using more of your midsection than lower-body turn, and try to get your shirt buttons in line with the ball as you make contact.

To find your ideal track, stand tall and point your right thumb out like a hitchhiker. Set your right elbow against your rib cage, just in front of the side seam on your shirt, and then fold your upper arm up without pulling your elbow off your rib cage. Check where your thumb points in relation to your right shoulder.

You're a low-track golfer if your thumb points below the top of your right shoulder. Your ideal clubhead path is defined by the plane that the shaft of your club sits on when you sole it on the ground at address (shaft plane).

You're a mid-track golfer if your thumb points even with the top of your right shoulder. Your ideal clubhead path, like Bradely's, is defined by the plane that extends from the target line through the tip of your right elbow at address (right-arm plane).

You're a high-track golfer if your thumb points above the top of your right shoulder. Your ideal clubhead path is defined by the plane that extends from the target line through your right shoulder at address.
—*Top 100 Teacher Mike Adams*

Try This! The Straight-Shot Finger Grip

Scan this photo *to watch a video of this lesson.*

Instead of wrapping your right index finger around the handle when you take your hold, point it straight down the right side of the grip and press it tightly against the handle [*photo, near right*]. This seemingly insignificant grip adjustment makes it almost impossible for your swing to break down at the end of your backswing. Usually the breakdown occurs because you overswing in situations that call for anything other than your run-of-the-mill iron swing or your grip isn't sound enough to stop your right wrist from collapsing at the top. Make sure to keep pressure from your right index finger on the handle the whole way. You know you're doing it right if it feels like you're in control of the club instead of the club controlling you.

—*Top 100 Teacher Rod Lidenberg*

Stop your slice by pressing your right index finger against the right side of the grip.

No! Breaking down at the top is a shotmaking no-no.

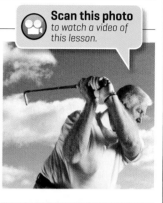

Yes! Use the finger grip to solidify your top position and ensure solid contact on any swing.

Pro Take Keegan Bradley on Letting Go

"If there's a theme to the advice on these pages, it's that the less you think, the better you'll overcome obstacles during your rounds and post better scores. Amateurs really need to learn how to separate practice from play. I know that's hard for a lot of golfers because there's not a lot of time to do both, but you won't hit your best shots in the clutch or from challenging lies if you're tinkering with your motion for 18 straight holes. Give my theory a go and see if it works. Play a full round without ever thinking about swing mechanics."

HOW TO PLAY THOUGHT FREE

1 *Get to the course earlier than you do now,* and treat that extra time as the practice session you never have time for. When your tee time is up, leave any swing thoughts on the range.

2 *Make a swing.* Don't try to hit the ball. There's a difference. Players who hit tend to stop their motions at impact. You're more likely to turn into a full finish when you swing. Simply let the ball get in the way.

3 *Don't talk shop.* You're with your buddies, who I'm sure aren't interested in your new weight-shift move to fix your reverse pivot. Start conversations on sports, cars, news—whatever. The less you think about the game and your swing, the more fun you'll have and the better you'll play.

STRAIGHT FROM THE SOURCE

Keegan on Keegan

"I think a lot of amateurs are tricked by what they see on TV. It looks like Tour players have smooth, flowing motions, but make no mistake—we swing fast. I won't blame you for wanting to feel smooth and relaxed when you're trying to hit an iron into a green in a clutch situation, but swinging slower than your natural pace can cause more problems than it fixes. Swing hard. In my opinion, less can go wrong when you try to rip it."

PLAY WITH FIRE

Here's the thing about trying to hit the ball hard: (1) It helps you be a little bit more athletic, and (2) it means that you have confidence in the club you've pulled and in the target you've chosen. The irons I hit into the 18th green, both in regulation and in the playoff, on the last day of the PGA Championship were hardly smooth. I gave them everything I had, and they were two of the best shots I hit all week.

THE RIGHT CLUB

If you're stuck between clubs, hit the lower club (an 8-iron instead of a 7-iron) and swing it harder. It's easier to ramp up speed and get good results than it is to dial it down.

MAINTAIN ANGLES

Stay in your address posture. This usually leads to good things, regardless of how fast or slow you're swinging. I won't get out of my address posture until I reach the finish like I am here.

STATS & SPECS

Bradley in the Rankings

Despite what many would consider standard technique, Keegan Bradley can reach swing speeds in excess of 120 mph. But it's really his versatility that keeps him in the game. Recent stats prove that he knows how to reach the green from a number of different lies at a clip that far outpaces his peers'.

Stats from 2012 season; courtesy of PGATour.com

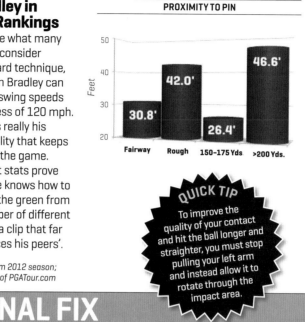

PROXIMITY TO PIN

Fairway	Rough	150–175 Yds.	>200 Yds.
30.8'	42.0'	26.4'	46.6'

Feet

QUICK TIP

To improve the quality of your contact and hit the ball longer and straighter, you must stop pulling your left arm and instead allow it to rotate through the impact area.

Keegan's Irons

Cleveland 588 MT
Clubs 4-iron through PW
Shaft True Temper Dynamic Gold [*X flex*]
Grips Lamkin

FINAL FIX

Build a Swing That Works Anywhere

Move your rib cage and arms in unison for sweeter contact

Properly coordinating your body movements is critical for solid ballstriking, but it isn't always easy to do. To simplify things, keep your rib cage and your arms aligned in four critical phases of your swing: address, transition, impact and release. In the photos at right, you can see that my arms and my rib cage are working as a team through the various phases of the swing and moving in unison from start to finish. The arms–rib cage relationship at address is almost identical to what's pictured in the other three photos, especially the one at impact. Add this coordination to your swing and you'll be more balanced and much more powerful.

—*Top 100 Teacher Kevin Kirk*

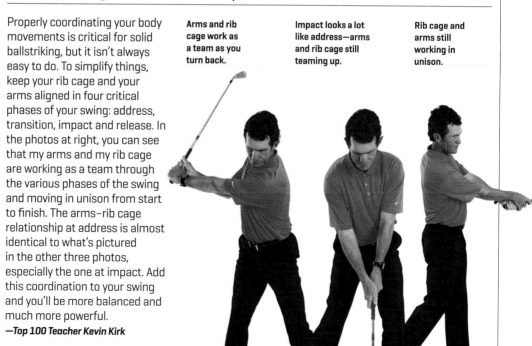

Arms and rib cage work as a team as you turn back.

Impact looks a lot like address—arms and rib cage still teaming up.

Rib cage and arms still working in unison.

With the help of the best short-game players on today's Tour, missing the green won't seem like such a big deal. In fact, your improved chipping, pitching and bunker techniques could become reliable scoring weapons for you, especially if you simultaneously work on your putting skills to make sure you hole out on your first attempt following a razor-sharp short shot. If you're serious about lowering your scores, copy the moves you see on the following pages step-by-step, because there's no faster route to saving par. Power hitters come and go, but the guys who know how to get up and down from anywhere and avoid three-putting at all costs are the ones who beat par for a lifetime.

To use the Scan-It/See-It feature in this section, look for the SCAN boxes (*example at right*). For instructions, see page 9. Videos also available at golf.com/plap.

Scan this photo to access bonus videos and lessons.

HOW TO PLAY LIKE...

- **Jim Furyk**
  Get his bunker swing
- **Nick Watney**
  Mimic his scrambling
- **Charles Howell III**
  Steal his chip swing
- **Matt Kuchar**
  Copy his pitch swing
- **Phil Mickelson**
  Get his creativity
- **Brandt Snedeker**
  Get his putting stroke
- **Zach Johnson**
  Learn his lag skills
- **Jason Day**
  Get his pure roll

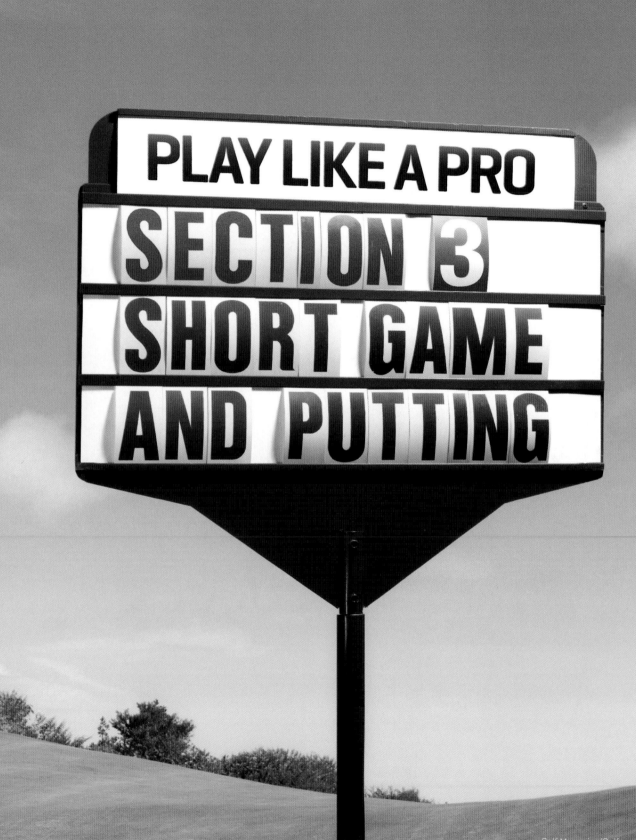

PLAY LIKE A PRO

SECTION 3

SHORT GAME

AND PUTTING

BUNKER SHOTS

Jim
Furyk

It's no surprise that the workmanlike Jim Furyk is one of the world's best at grinding out par from greenside sand. With steely reserve and a knack for taking the right kind of sand divot, Furyk does what all great bunker players, past and present, have always done: use the sand to propel the ball onto the green.

Tour veteran Jim Furyk is an outstanding all-around player, but his No. 1 skill compared with his peers is getting it close from greenside sand.

SKILL BREAKDOWN

"This is one of the few times in golf where you're actually required to hit too far behind the ball." —Mike Malaska

Pro File

Jim Furyk

Full name James Michael Furyk
Born May 12, 1970
Birthplace West Chester, Pa.
Residence Ponte Vedra Beach, Fla.
Height / Weight 6' 2" / 185 lbs.
College University of Arizona
Turned professional 1992
Professional victories 26 (16 PGA Tour)*
Majors 2003 U.S. Open*
Career U.S. earnings $53.7 million*

*Through 2013 U.S. Open

You're vexed by bunkers. You're not really sure how you should address the ball in sand, how hard a swing to make or where to make contact. Truth is, you're making things hard on yourself by overthinking the situation. All good bunker players, especially those on the same elite level as Jim Furyk, know that the secret to getting the ball out of sand is getting sand out of the bunker.

If you're like most golfers, you're afraid to make a big swing in sand because the ball might fly too far. After all, you're right next to the green, and a full swing is *waaaay* too much power, right? Wrong. This is one of the few times in golf where you're actually required to hit too far behind the ball. Your target at the bottom of your swing is the sand behind the ball, not the ball itself. And sand is heavy. On most sand shots, you'll displace a full cup of sand. That's a significant amount of weight, which is why you need to free up your backswing and come down with good acceleration to launch the sand and the ball out of the bunker. Cut your backswing short or slow down as your clubhead approaches impact and you'll likely be hitting your next shot from the sand, too.

Simplify things by taking your normal stance and making your full normal swing. **The only key adjustment is to open your clubface when the ball is sitting up, square it if the ball is partly submerged, and hood it if the ball is buried.** Each of these clubface positions results in displacing a different amount of sand when your club enters and swings through the bunker. An open face takes less sand, and a closed face takes more.
—*Top 100 Teacher Mike Malaska, Superstition Mountain G.C., Superstition Mountain, Ariz.*

Rank File

PGA Tour Sand Save Percentage	
2007	50.9%
2008	50.7%
2009	54.6%
2010	48.0%
2011	53.5%
2012	65.2%
2013	54.6%*

*Through May

Stats courtesy of PGATour.com

No!

The ball isn't riding on a cushion of sand; it's riding in it! The benefits of the loft built into your sand wedge are gone.

No!

This is a great clubhead position for a full swing, where you want to release the club, but this ball is going to come up short.

Yes!

Even this deep into the swing, the face is still flat—zero hand manipulation. The ball is up and headed to the green.

Yes!

Swing your arms, not your hands, to keep the face from shutting down. If you can hold the face steady through impact like this, you're going to land the ball on the green every time.

Try This! **Soften Up Your Sand Shots**

The easiest way to hit a soft bunker shot is to slow the clubhead down just as it reaches impact. You probably do this already by either decelerating or simply sticking the clubhead deep into the sand, but these methods typically result in the ball staying in the bunker. Instead you should use my one-hand technique, in which you allow your right hand to come off the club as you pass through impact.

Step 1 Assume your normal setup with your weight slightly left, the clubface a bit open and the ball forward in your stance.
Step 2 Make your normal swing, but let go of the grip with your right hand just as the clubhead makes contact with the sand.
Step 3 Finish the shot with your left hand only, but don't stop your swing. The ball should come out softly and stop quickly.
—Top 100 Teacher Shawn Humphries

Scan this photo to watch a video of this lesson.

STRAIGHT FROM THE SOURCE

Furyk on Furyk

"I've had a lot of success from greenside bunkers over the years, because I have confidence in my technique. The secret is to know how to hit every bunker shot, not just your standard run-of-the-mill blast. The most difficult shot you'll face is the bunker blast from a downslope. Here's where you can add strokes in a hurry, turning a good round into just an average one. It's a shot you'll have to practice, because normal preparations won't do. Here's how I handle golf's toughest shot. I call it that because the slope will take loft off your club, and loft is critical for greenside bunker success."

ADDRESS

Take a wider stance than usual to keep your balance. The key is to align your shoulders with the slope. Once you do that, open the clubface and make your normal bunker swing.

SWING

The big error here is swinging too hard or cutting under the ball too much. That's when you hit a screaming skull that ends up in a bunker on the other side of the green. Try to hinge the club along the slope rather than overswinging your arms and shoulders.

STATS & SPECS

Furyk vs. the Field Not only did Jim Furyk lead the PGA Tour in Sand Saves in 2012, he led the pro circuit in Proximity to the Pin from Sand as well. Incredibly, Furyk landed his 94 greenside bunker shots that year an average of 6' 11" from the hole.

Stats from 2012 season; courtesy of PGATour.com

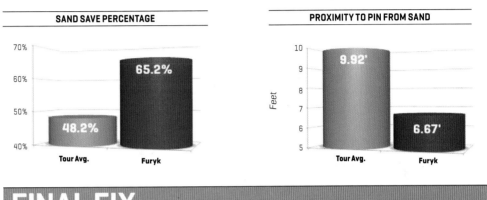

SAND SAVE PERCENTAGE

Tour Avg.	48.2%
Furyk	65.2%

PROXIMITY TO PIN FROM SAND

Feet

Tour Avg.	9.92'
Furyk	6.67'

IMPACT

Bring the club back to the ball on a line parallel with the slope and continue on the path as you blast through the sand under the ball. The ball will come out lower and with less spin than if you were on a level lie, so plan for the extra roll.

FINAL FIX

The Best Drill for Your Sand Game

Make a ridge in the practice bunker and then thump it

Scan this photo to watch a video of this lesson.

In a good bunker swing you use your wedge to blast sand onto the green, and the sand carries the ball out of the bunker. The first part is the most important—your wedge hits the hazard, not the ball. The trick is to get the second part right by taking the right amount of sand. Here's a drill that will help you nail your blast every time.

Step 1 Drop a ball in the practice bunker, then use the back of a bunker rake to create a five-foot-long ridge of sand from the ball to the far side of the hazard.

Step 2 Starting at the far side of the ridge, take your stance with your weight favoring your left side and with an open stance, and make your swing.

Step 3 Check your blast mark in the sand—it should be centered over the ridge, not before or after [*right*].

Step 4 Take a step toward the ball and make your swing again, and keep stepping and swinging until you get to the ball. By that time you should have grooved the motion you need to take the right-sized divot. This is a very helpful drill because it shifts your focus from the ball to the sand, which is your true target. And the ridge allows you to really feel your wedge sliding—not shoveling—through the sand. If you do it correctly you'll hear a soft *thump* sound as the sole of your wedge impacts the sand. That's the sound of bunker-shot success.
—Top 100 Teacher Carol Preisinger

TOO EARLY

TOO LATE

JUST RIGHT

TARGET →

Nick **Watney**

You may know Nick Watney as the guy with the 121-mph driver swing, but you don't amass a sub-71 career scoring average with distance alone. Over the past several seasons, Watney has worked hard to develop an elite short game, something that always comes in handy when your big shots turn into big misses.

After learning the new way to swing wedges with Top 100 Teacher James Sieckmann, Nick Watney became one of the PGA Tour's most adept scramblers.

SKILL BREAKDOWN

"Your short-game downswing is little more than letting the clubhead fall back to the ball in a circle."

—James Sieckmann

ince I began working with Nick beginning in 2010, I've tried to simplify his short swings for easier up-and-downs using the following, proven keys:

STANCE Set your back foot square to your target line and flare your front foot. Opening up like this moves the low point of your swing in front of the ball, exactly where it should be.

PLANE The most efficient way to deliver the club to the ball on a short shot is to swing the clubshaft and clubhead on the plane line established by the lie angle at address.

ENERGY Good wedge players move their head toward the target a few inches during the backswing; then they either keep their head still or move it even farther forward in the downswing. This gets energy flowing toward the target—a must for solid contact.

SWING Your short-game downswing is little more than letting the clubhead fall back to the ball in a circle and then turning your chest to support the motion of the club.

RELEASE You shouldn't "hold" on to your release by keeping your hands ahead of the clubhead past impact. Doing this destroys your rhythm and feel and invites digging.

CLUBFACE As you swing the club back on plane, let the clubface rotate open. An open clubface lets you release the club properly without fear of hitting the ball left.
—*Top 100 Teacher James Sieckmann, Shadow Ridge C.C., Omaha, Nebr.*

SKILL PRACTICE

If you can hit solid chips using only your right arm, then you have the feel for the finesse sequence found in all great short swings.

Scan this photo to watch a video of this lesson.

Clubhead goes first...

...followed by the right arm...

...and supported by the chest and hips.

The New Way to Hit Wedge Shots

Learn how to finesse wedge shots instead of powering them using the old technique

By Top 100 Teacher **JAMES SIECKMANN**, *Shadow Ridge C.C., Omaha, Nebr.*

The new way to hit wedge shots comes down to changing the sequence in your downswing so that the club moves faster than your arms in the transition, then learning how to support the movement of the club with your arms and chest. To do this, try hitting shots with only your right arm (or your left, if you're a southpaw). I know it sounds simplistic, but hitting solid shots this way automatically creates the correct sequence in your

swing, without any thinking on your part. In other words, you must swing in the proper clubhead-leading-the-body motion or you'll hit fat or thin shots. As you perform this drill, focus on the following:

1 Get the clubhead moving first. The club accelerates first and fastest, followed by your arms, chest and, finally, your hips. (Yes, this sequence is the exact opposite of what you use in full swings.)

2 Turn your chest through impact. This supports the

release of the club and ensures that you don't stop your arm swing at impact. Continue to swing your right arm past your body and smoothly accelerate the clubhead past your hands. You'll know you did it

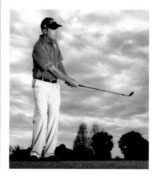

correctly if, at the finish, the grip points at your belly and the face is slightly open.

3 Place your left hand on the grip while holding your finish. In order to fit your left hand on the handle, you'll have to fold your left elbow and cup your left wrist. (Look for wrinkles on the back of your left wrist.) These are key moves to correctly release the clubhead and optimize loft and bounce.

Add your left hand to the handle at the end of the drill for a more realistic feel of the proper swing and finish.

SKILL ANALYSIS

WATCH & LEARN SWING WITH FINESSE, NOT POWER

In a power swing, you want to generate as much speed as possible—loft and bounce are unimportant. In a finesse swing you want to *control* speed and exploit loft and bounce. There's a change in mechanics as well as a switch in the way you mentally approach each swing.

The role of your lower body on short shots is to provide stability and balance. You don't use it to create power. Notice how Nick Watney, a Sieckmann student since 2010, initiates his downward movement by moving the club first, before his body. Think of it as a gentle casting motion or, in other words, letting gravity be your friend. **You can see how Watney's hips don't really turn until after the club gets back in front of his body.**

The feeling you're after is to have soft and relaxed arms that swing the club past your lower body while your chest smoothly rotates toward the target at the same pace. If you hit your 5-iron this way, the ball would go nowhere. Essentially, great wedge players are weak on purpose.
—*Top 100 Teacher James Sieckmann*

Head has moved toward the target during the backswing. Not often taught, but it's the right way to get energy moving toward the target.

Arms moving faster than the lower body and the club moving faster than the hands. This is the new way to hit wedge shots.

Lower body stable and chest rotating with the arm swing to support the momentum of the club.

Clubhead releasing, heel over toe. This is the signature finish of all great short-game players.

STATS & SPECS

Watney in the Rankings

The numbers show that Watney is steadily increasing his rank in all scrambling areas, but the most eye opening is the Scrambling percentage itself. After learning the new ways to swing wedges, Watney jumped 134 spots in the Tour Scrambling rank, from a dismal 146th in 2010 to a sparkling 12th in 2011.

134

Watney's rise in Scrambling rank from 2010 to 2011.

QUICK TIP
Just like you do on longer approaches, adjust for shot length on short pitches and chips by making your backswing shorter or longer. Never alter pace or swing speed.

Watney's Wedges

Nike VR Pro
PW 49 degrees
SW 55 degrees
LW 59 degrees

4

Clubhead moving back to the ball on plane. No need to cut across the ball or swing out to the right.

8

12

FINAL FIX

Tilt Your Head on Chip Shots

This easy setup trick ensures crisp contact

When preparing to hit a chip shot you make a critical mistake at address: You tilt your head and set your right eye closer to the ground than your left. This error immediately puts you in a setup that not only makes it difficult to control distance, but also makes solid contact highly unlikely.

To remedy this problem, tilt your head in the opposite direction so that your left eye is closer to the ground than your right—just an inch or so. This very simple alteration will naturally shift more of your weight toward your front foot and aim the back of your left hand more toward the target.

Compare the photos at left and right and notice how much more level my shoulders are with my left eye closer to the ground than my right. That's a good thing when chipping. Make this move and you'll have a much easier time striking the ball with a slightly descending blow, pinching it cleanly between the clubface and the ground rather than scooping it on the upswing.
—*Top 100 Teacher Martin Hall*

No! *Right eye closer to the ground than left eye.*

Yes! *Tilt your head so that your left eye is closer to the ground than your right for improved chipping.*

Charles
Howell III

Absent from PGA Tour leader boards for the past several seasons, Charles Howell III has rededicated himself to mastering the short game, and it's paying off with a rise up the chipping stats ledger and a barrage of Top 10 finishes. For Howell, and every other Tour pro, scoring begins from 20 yards and in.

By altering his setup to match the situation he's facing, Charles Howell III has become a chipping and scrambling savant.

SKILL BREAKDOWN

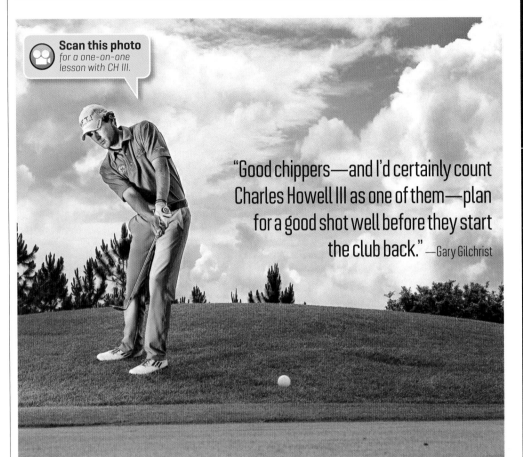

Scan this photo for a one-on-one lesson with CH III.

"Good chippers—and I'd certainly count Charles Howell III as one of them—plan for a good shot well before they start the club back." —Gary Gilchrist

Hitting a poor chip is like missing a short putt—they're both strokes that are gone forever. Short chip shots are meant to be easy, yet the majority of recreational players fail to land them close enough to the pin for an easy up-and-down. Their problems stem from a lack of preparation—not that you don't practice enough. It's more that you're practicing the wrong things and rely too much on technique to hit a successful shot.

Good chippers—and I'd certainly count Charles Howell III as one of them—plan for a good chip shot well before they start the club back. Contact is king on short chips, and the only reliable method for ensuring a solid and controlled strike is matching your setup to the situation you're facing. For any chip, Howell will alter stance width, weight distribution, ball position, swing length and wrist set to not only increase the likelihood of ball-first contact, but also to fine-tune trajectory and distance, depending on his lie and yardage to the pin.

Basically, the more you hinge your wrists, the higher and farther you'll chip the ball (and vice versa). The more you position the ball back in your stance and set weight on your front foot, the lower you'll chip the ball (and vice versa).

The best advice I can give you is to spend a few hours at your short-game practice facility and experiment with various setups and swing lengths and see what they give you. (Look for carry distance, roll distance and total distance on each one.) If you can find the setup recipe for three specific chip shots—say, 5, 10 and 15 yards with equal parts carry and roll—you'll be well ahead of the other members of your foursome.
—*Top 100 Teacher Gary Gilchrist, Gary Gilchrist Golf Academy, Howey-in-the-Hills, Fla.*

SKILL PRACTICE

Halve the distance between you and the green to determine the best landing spot—and shot trajectory—for every chip you face.

Scan this photo *to watch a video of this lesson.*

If you're two paces off the green...

...land the chip one pace on the green.

How to Hit Can't-Miss Chips

Choose the right landing area to get the right trajectory for the shot at hand

**By Top 100 Teacher
DOM DiJULIA,** *Jericho National G.C., New Hope, Pa.*

Selecting the best shot to handle the short-game situation you're facing is a matter of deciding the right trajectory and landing area. The two work hand-in-hand—your landing area and its position relative to where the hole is located tell you how high or low to hit

the shot. Picking the landing spot comes first. You options are as follows:

1 Pick a spot close to the hole, but this requires you to fly the ball the whole way—not a high-percentage shot.

2 Pick a spot near the fringe of the green, but if you come up short, you'll be hitting a second chip. Not good when you need to save par.

3 Use my foolproof spot-selection guide, which gives you the perfect combo of carry and roll to snuggle the ball close to the pin.

It's easy—walk off the distance between your lie and the edge of the green. Halve that distance, and that's how far you should land the ball on the green. For example, if you're six paces off the green, plan to land the ball three paces

on the green. When you see where you need to land the ball and the distance from that spot to the hole, you'll instinctively figure out the trajectory that the shot requires to get it close. As you practice this technique, you'll find that the resulting shot gives you the perfect blend of a high success rate with a high margin for error. That'll pay huge dividends over the long run.

SKILLS ANALYSIS

Scan this photo to see CH III's chip swing in pure slow motion.

Weight slightly forward, ball slightly back, shaft leaning toward target.

Left arm continually moving toward the target at an even pace.

Left wrist perfectly flat at the point of impact.

WATCH & LEARN TOUR-STYLE CHIP STROKE

As with most shots, you can eliminate the majority of your errors if you make sure your setup is correct. The goal of your chipping address position is to situate your body, arms, hands and club to create a descending blow without chunking the clubhead into the ground or striking the ball with the leading edge of the clubface. I recommend that you stand far enough away from the

ball that you can bend forward from your hips and get your chest over your toes. Do it correctly and you'll feel like your arms are hanging straight down without touching your torso or your legs. Set the majority of your weight over your left foot, and try to keep it there during your stroke. If your weight moves to your right foot, you'll likely catch the chip thin.

When you go to make your stroke, copy Howell's technique and think of it as an elongated putt. Swing the club back using the triangle formed by your shoulders and arms. **A bit of wrist hinge is okay to add some feel to the shot, but as you strike the ball you want your left wrist to be as flat as possible.** Keep the triangle—and, specifically, your left arm—moving all the way through

Club powered by the triangle formed by the shoulders and arms.

A touch of wrist hinge for enhanced touch and feel.

Left arm stays straight and moves past his left leg.

Scan this photo *to watch a video of this lesson.*

the shot. Stopping movement leads to deceleration and a poor result and encourages flipping the clubhead at the ball through the hitting zone. If you copy the positions shown in the above swing sequence, you'll get the majority of your chips into tap-in range and save par more often than not.
—*Top 100 Teacher Kellie Stenzel, Palm Beach G.C., Palm Beach, Fla.*

Try This! Recoil on Short Chips

Try to think of the chipping stroke as a short, crisp move that creates a "pop" at impact. To make this happen, use your normal stroke, but instead of allowing the club to follow through after impact and hinge up into your release, bring it back to your initial backswing position. The club should feel as though it's recoiling after impact, which will give you the sensation of a lively, crisp, short stroke. This will encourage a much more aggressive downswing, which is key for crispness.
—*Top 100 Teacher Rick McCord*

STRAIGHT FROM THE SOURCE

Howell on Howell

"Even for us Tour pros, a short-side chip with little room between the ball and the pin is a dicey situation. The tendency is to baby these shots too much and come up well short, then add too much speed the next time you face a delicate chip and blow it to the other side of the green. As I do on all short-game shots, I use my setup to guarantee the correct contact, trajectory and distance. Copy what you see here and you'll not only chip short shots closer, a few of them may start to go in."

QUICK TIP

Ditch your wedge and chip the ball with one of your hybrids. The design of these clubs makes it easier to catch the ball cleanly and get it rolling purely toward the hole.

SETUP

On short chips I strive for neutrality: ball slightly back, weight slightly forward and hands slightly ahead of the clubhead.

BACKSWING

I like to feel firm-wristed on short chips. I'll preset a little wrist cock at address and then hold it going back. I avoid hinging on the way back because it forces you to unhinge coming down, and that's when you can over- or underaccelerate.

THROUGH-SWING

Since I haven't added any hinge on the way back I simply swing them through, supporting their movement with just a touch of body turn. I want my arms and club to feel like a single unit and swing them as far past the ball as I did on my backswing.

STATS & SPECS

Howell vs. the Field

Since working with Top 100 Teacher Gary Gilchrist, Charles Howell III has made eye-popping strides in his short game. Check the improvement from 2012 to 2013 in the charts at right. With these numbers, Howell has jumped 113 spots in the Scrambling statistical category during the same time period.

2013 stats through Memorial Tournament

Stats courtesy of PGATour.com

2012 SCRAMBLING

Tour Avg. 63.3%
Howell III 60.0%

2013 SCRAMBLING

Tour Avg. 65.2%
Howell III 83.2%

Mizuno MP T-4

GW 52 degrees
[7 degree bounce]
SW 56 degrees
[13 degree bounce]
LW 58 degrees
[bent to 60 degrees]

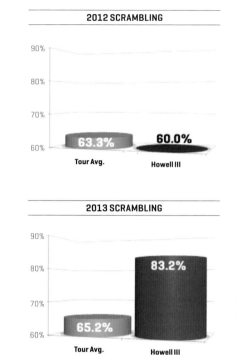

FINAL FIX

A Drill for Sweet Chips

Swing with your body for better short-shot control

For fewer fat and thin chips, learn the feeling of releasing the club with your body rather than flipping it with your hands. The following drill can really help:

Step 1 Grip your wedge halfway down the shaft and get into your address position, placing the handle on your left hip.

Step 2 Move the club away by rotating your right forearm—the toe of the club should move up, while the handle moves down. Stop when the shaft is parallel to your target line.

Step 3 Rotate the club back around your body toward impact, but do it by rotating your arms and chest together, not by flipping your hands. If the handle of the club hits your left side, you've released the club too much with your hands. If the shaft doesn't touch your side, you've successfully released the club with your body.

—*Top 100 Teacher Brad Brewer*

Yes! Start here.

Yes! Finish here.

Skill No. 13
PITCH SHOTS

Rain or shine, Matt Kuchar is a safe bet to knock short-but-tough pitch shots close to the hole.

Matt
Kuchar

With a game devoid of weak spots, it's not often Matt Kuchar needs to rely on his short game to keep his scores in the red. When he does, however, he breaks out time-proven fundamentals to knock tough pitches close with impressive regularity. Make his keys your keys.

SKILL BREAKDOWN

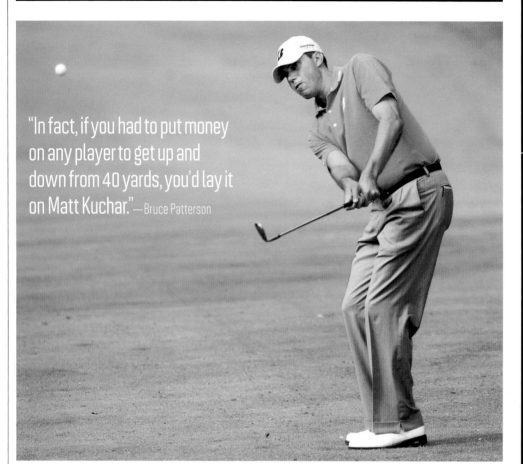

"In fact, if you had to put money on any player to get up and down from 40 yards, you'd lay it on Matt Kuchar." —Bruce Patterson

To say that Matt Kuchar knows how to pitch the ball close is a huge understatement. He's consistently in the Top 15 in the Scrambling statistic category and is an expert at judging how the ball will behave once it hits the green. In fact, if you had to put money on any player to get up and down from 40 yards, you'd lay it on Matt Kuchar. His performance abilities from short range are the polar opposite of the ones executed by amateurs, the majority of whom have no clue how to create the right trajectory and distance for expert pitches.

The key to solid pitch shots is taking the club away by rotating your left forearm clockwise while also turning your chest away from the ball. This combination of movements keeps the club from getting too far inside and also prevents the clubface from rotating closed. Once you get this part of your pitch swing down, all that's left to do is to simply move your chest and forearm down to the ball together. This will stop you from flipping the clubhead through impact and make the quality of your contact much more solid. Here's a quick rundown:

1 Take your normal setup and then rotate your left forearm to your right. Your left elbow should face the target and the clubface should be open.
2 Rotate your chest away from the ball without moving your arms independently. This will take the club back to a solid on-plane position.
3. Move your arms and chest back down together without any "hit" with your arms or hands. Let the heel of the club pass through the turf before the toe.
—*Top 100 Teacher Bruce Patterson, Butler National G.C., Oak Brook, Ill.*

SKILL PRACTICE

How to Stop Pitch Shots with Spin

Here's the pro way to make the ball bite after a single hop

By Top 100 Teacher **BRIAN MANZELLA**, English Turn Golf & C.C., New Orleans, La.

When you find yourself in an awkward pitching position where you need extra spin to keep the ball from rolling too much after it hits the green, you don't know how to handle it. Your current technique is to hit down on the ball with a steep angle of attack in the hope of catching the ball first and producing a high-spinning shot that stops quickly near the hole. Unfortunately, this technique typically leads to chunks that only travel a few yards or thin shots that rocket over the green.

Instead of hitting down steeply on the ball, you need to shallow-out your approach. To do this, feel that your arms are moving faster than your torso (but still staying soft and supple) as they swing down and through impact. This move will force your arms to suck in to your body as they swing through impact (*photo, top right*), creating a much flatter, shallower angle of attack into the ball. In fact, you might feel the clubhead touch the grass just before it strikes the ball because of the shallow angle of your swing. If you do it right, you'll hit the ball on a low spot on the clubface, which will create a low launch angle with shot-stopping spin.

Scan this photo to watch a video of this lesson.

Let your arms suck in to your body after impact to beat those tricky in-between yardages.

Create a shallow angle of attack to launch the ball lower and with plenty of spin.

Use an aggressive swing and allow the clubhead to pass your hands through impact.

Your arms will naturally suck in to your body if you move them faster than your body.

STRAIGHT FROM THE SOURCE

WATCH & LEARN ROTATE THE CLUB TO VARY YOUR SPIN

When faced with pitch shots around the green, most amateurs only have one basic shot and don't have the ability to alter how the ball reacts when it lands. You're too limited in your shot selection to be able to get close to certain pins or deal with varying conditions. You need to expand your repertoire immediately.

The simple way pros like Matt Kuchar control pitch shots is to alter the way they rotate, or don't rotate, the clubhead as they swing into the finish. **There are three different positions you need to master to generate three different kinds of short-game shots.** Check them out below.

—*Top 100 Teacher Dom DiJulia, Jericho National G.C., New Hope, Pa.*

QUICK TIP
Simplify your backswing by hinging the club up with your wrists. That's it. You'll create plenty of potential energy to pitch the ball up to 30 yards without having to swing your arms.

STANDARD PITCH

Finish your swing with the toe of your wedge pointing straight into the air. Getting into this kind of finish position creates a neutral shot (no excess carry, spin or roll) that's good for a variety of situations. This is the one you'll want as your default short-game shot.

SPINNING PITCH

For extra shot-stopping spin, hold off your release so that the toe points to the right of vertical in the finish (about 2 o'clock on a clock face). This less-rotated position promotes extra spin and stopping power (as well as more loft) on your shots, which is great for getting at front pins and stopping the ball quickly on downslopes and fast greens.

Scan this photo
to watch a video of this lesson.

STATS & SPECS

Kuchar vs. the Field

From roughly 30 yards around the green, Matt Kuchar was a tough man to beat in 2012, pitching the ball roughly 24 percent closer than the average proximity to the pin from that range. The key to this stat is that the make percentage of the putt from Kuchar's leave is 46 percent; from the average Tour leave it's 29.8 percent.

Stats from 2012 season; courtesy of PGATour.com

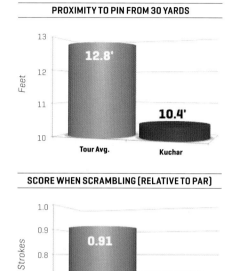

PROXIMITY TO PIN FROM 30 YARDS

Feet

- Tour Avg. — 12.8'
- Kuchar — 10.4'

SCORE WHEN SCRAMBLING (RELATIVE TO PAR)

Strokes

- Tour Avg. — 0.91
- Kuchar — 0.72

ROLL-OUT PITCH

Point the toe left of vertical when you finish. To picture the proper position, think of the toe pointing at around 10 o'clock on a clock face (from your perspective). This slightly more rotated position will create shots that release when they hit the green and is great for reaching back pins and climbing uphill slopes.

FINAL FIX

Rain Pitch Shots on Your Targets

My umbrella drill gives you a feel for perfect pitches

Open your golf umbrella and set it into the ground, handle up. Take 10 balls and drop them about 30 yards from the umbrella. Using your regular pitch motion, try to land as many balls in the umbrella as possible. As you do this, you'll quickly learn how to adjust your swing (i.e., make it longer, shorter, faster or slower) and start rattling balls into the bottom of the umbrella. After hitting 10 balls from 30 yards, move to 40 yards, then 50 yards and so on.

The umbrella drill works because it gives you a nice big target and gets you in the habit of hitting to an area rather than to a precise spot, which adds tension. It also provides a reward for good shots, which will help you practice longer and remain focused on the task at hand. (Challenge a friend and make a game of it to get even more from the drill.) And you're almost certain to see that umbrella instead of the flag the next time you hit a pitch during a round, and your experience with it will help you knock the ball close, just as you did in your practice.

—Top 100 Teacher Nancy Quarcelino

Scan this photo to watch a video of this lesson.

Skill No. 14
CREATIVITY

Phil
Mickelson

Equipped with impeccable technique, an arsenal of savvy shots and a flair for the dramatic, Phil Mickelson has become synonymous with short-game creativity. In fact, Lefty is at his best when he misses greens. Here's how to get his touch and confidence and start seeing tough short shots as legitimate scoring options, not fast tracks to bogey and worse.

Phil Mickelson has never faced a tricky short shot he didn't like. Confidence and an ability to imagine different trajectories and ball flights have made him a true short-game artist.

SKILL BREAKDOWN

"'Feel' players like Mickelson know what the clubhead is doing at every point in the swing." —Mike Adams

Phil Mickeslon

Full name Phil Alfred Mickelson
Nickname Lefty
Born June 16, 1970
Birthplace San Diego, Calif.
Residence Rancho Santa Fe, Calif.
Height / Weight 6' 3" / 200 lbs.
College Arizona State University
Turned professional 1992
Professional victories 49 (41 PGA Tour)*
Majors 2004, 2006, 2010 Masters; 2005 PGA Championship*
Career U.S. earnings $71.1 million*

*Through 2013 U.S. Open

Rank File

PGA Tour Short Game Stats
Proximity to the Hole from Around the Green

Year	Proximity	
2007	6' 9"	(18th)
2008	6' 8"	(15th)
2009	6' 6"	(13th)
2010	6' 8"	(25th)
2011	6' 8"	(14th)
2012	6' 10"	(25th)

Stats courtesy of PGATour.com

Caution: Magician at work. That's the warning sign posted next to Phil Mickelson's bag whenever he's hitting a short shot into the green, although Phil rarely heeds the warnings. More apt to take the high-risk-high-reward route than play the safest shot onto the green, Mickelson's game has come to define the creativity needed to save par from challenging short-game situations. It's eye-popping and nothing short of amazing.

One thing that Mickelson does better than most players is swing with smooth acceleration regardless of the type of short shot he's hitting. Most golfers tend to make jabby, all-arms swings with little feel for plane, shift and release. You'd be better served treating short shots as miniature full swings. A lighter grip would probably help, too. "Feel" players like Mickelson know what the clubhead is doing at every point in the swing.

One way to get this type of control is to use a lighter grip pressure when you're hitting soft pitches into the green (a 7 on a 1-to-10 scale instead of your usual 10). The moment you grip the handle too tightly is the moment your hands stop sensing what the clubhead is doing.

Phil Mickelson can hit thousands of different short game shots, even ones he's never seen before, because he's so good at visualization. It's critical that you build an image of the type of shot you want to hit (how high it will go and what it will do once it hits the ground). Your eyes are powerful tools—they send signals to your brain that tell it how you should move. It's up to you to ultimately hit the shot, but don't underestimate the power of imagination.
—Top 100 Teacher Mike Adams, The Medalist Club, Hobe Sound, Fla., and Hamilton Farm G.C., Gladstone, N.J.

SKILL PRACTICE

Allow the clubhead to pass your hands as you swing through impact, so that the grip again points behind your zipper.

Scan this photo to watch a video of this lesson.

The Easy Way to Hit Lefty's Flop

My secret: Keep your hands behind your zipper until after impact

By Top 100 Teacher
JIM MURPHY, *Sugar Creek C.C.,*
Sugar Land, Tex.

When you try to hit high, soft lob shots, you either slam the clubhead down into the turf or blade the ball across the green. You also tend to place your hands well forward at address, thinking that it'll help you slide under the ball, but all it does is make it nearly impossible to execute the shot you want. You need to correct your setup before you have any chance of playing a reliable lob shot.

First, set up with more weight on your front foot and your hands positioned behind the clubhead so that the grip points slightly behind your zipper (*photo, right*). This will hinge your left wrist away from the target and lean the grip of the club in the same direction. Although setting up with the grip of the club leaning away from the target might seem counterintuitive, it makes it much easier to let the clubhead pass your hands through impact, which is critical for creating a high, lofted shot (*photo, above*). Make sure you don't slide your head or body past the ball as you swing down into impact.

Set your hands and the butt of the club behind your zipper at address.

SKILL ANALYSIS

WATCH & LEARN ROUGH ESCAPES

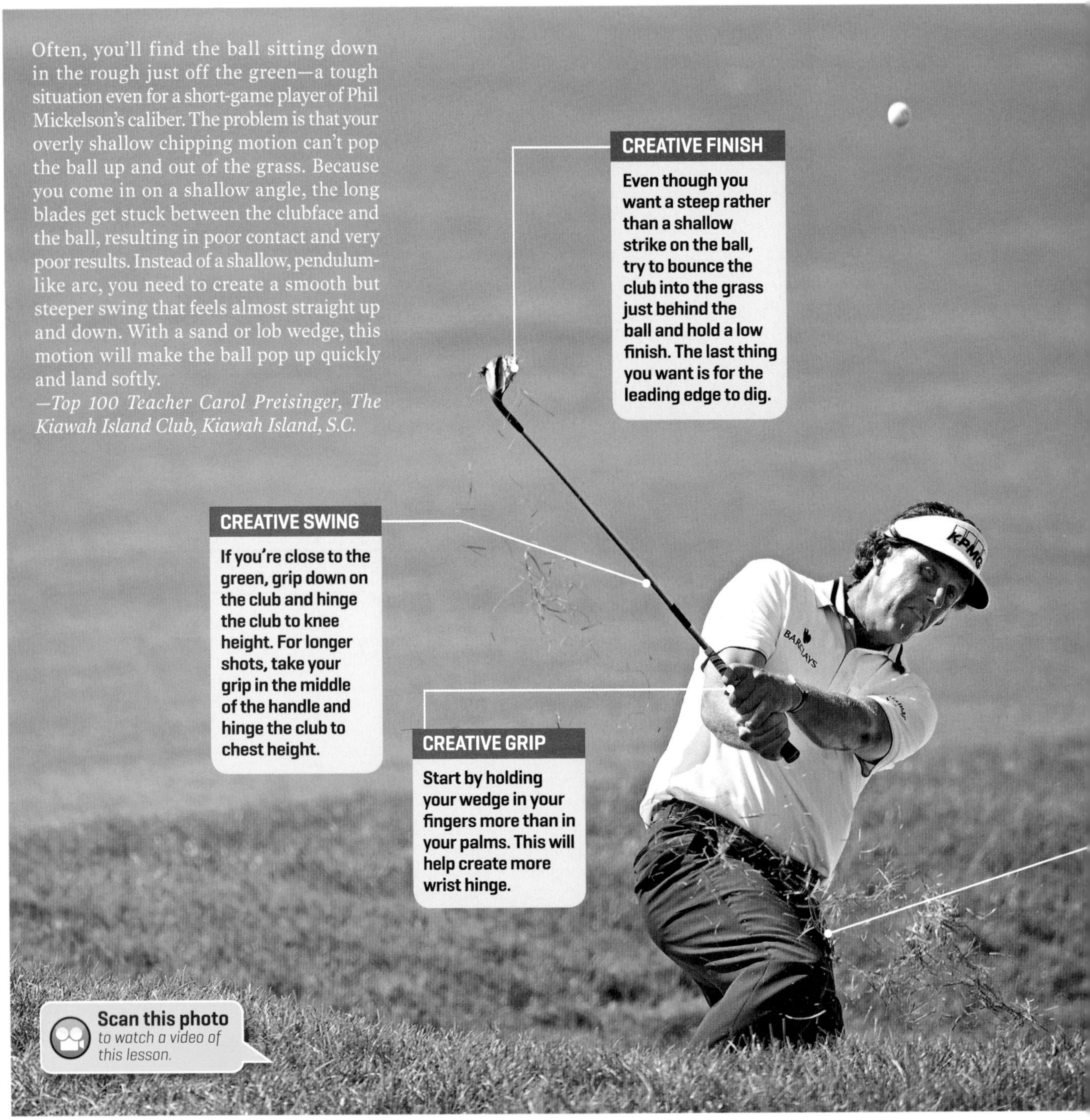

Often, you'll find the ball sitting down in the rough just off the green—a tough situation even for a short-game player of Phil Mickelson's caliber. The problem is that your overly shallow chipping motion can't pop the ball up and out of the grass. Because you come in on a shallow angle, the long blades get stuck between the clubface and the ball, resulting in poor contact and very poor results. Instead of a shallow, pendulum-like arc, you need to create a smooth but steeper swing that feels almost straight up and down. With a sand or lob wedge, this motion will make the ball pop up quickly and land softly.

—Top 100 Teacher Carol Preisinger, The Kiawah Island Club, Kiawah Island, S.C.

CREATIVE FINISH

Even though you want a steep rather than a shallow strike on the ball, try to bounce the club into the grass just behind the ball and hold a low finish. The last thing you want is for the leading edge to dig.

CREATIVE SWING

If you're close to the green, grip down on the club and hinge the club to knee height. For longer shots, take your grip in the middle of the handle and hinge the club to chest height.

CREATIVE GRIP

Start by holding your wedge in your fingers more than in your palms. This will help create more wrist hinge.

Scan this photo *to watch a video of this lesson.*

STATS & SPECS

Mickelson vs. the Field

Even in his 21st year on Tour, Phil Mickelson remains one of the game's elite short-shot players. His creativity has helped him amass 41 PGA Tour wins while keeping him competitive during a time in his career when touch typically falters.

Stats from 2012 season; courtesy of PGATour.com

SCRAMBLING PERCENTAGE

- Tour Avg.
- Mickelson

65%
60%
55%
50%

From Sand · From Rough · From Other Locations

QUICK TIP
The trick to getting extra loft on delicate short shots around the green and hitting a Mickelson-esque flop? Allow your left wrist to cup though impact and hold the cup into the finish.

Lefty's Wedges

Callaway JAWS
GW 52 degrees
LW 60 degrees
XW 64 degrees

FINAL FIX

"Bounce" Your Short Shots

Use more sole and less leading edge for sweeter short-shot contact

When you chip, you tend to lean the shaft toward the target with your hands ahead of the ball at address, thinking that this will give you the downward strike you need to catch the ball crisply. However, leaning the shaft too far forward affects the natural face progression built into the club and moves the leading edge of your wedge closer to the ground. With the lead edge positioned so close to the turf, you're almost guaranteed to dig too much into the grass and hit the shot fat.

The smart play is to play the ball in the middle of your stance and set your hands almost in line with your zipper. This exposes the full amount of bounce built into your wedge so you can swing under and through the ball and strike it crisply without digging into the ground. When you see Tour players lean the shaft forward, it's almost always because they're hitting something other than a standard chip. For most amateurs, using the maximum amount of bounce by keeping the shaft vertical at address is the way to go.
—*Top 100 Teacher Fred Griffin*

CREATIVE STANCE

Open your stance (which will also promote a steep takeaway) and play the ball a bit farther forward to take full advantage of the bounce on your wedge.

Shaft near vertical for maximum bounce.

Shaft leaning slightly forward, lessening bounce and increasing dig.

Shaft leaning excessively forward—dig impending.

Skill No. 15
PUTT CONTROL

With his "pop" style putting stroke, Snedeker is about as old-school as it gets on the greens, but his results are setting new standards for putting excellence.

Brandt
Snedeker

An old-school stroke and one of the quickest "read-to-putt" times around have helped Brandt Snedeker amass a jaw-dropping percentage of one-putts over the past several seasons, solidifying his reputation as the best putter on Tour. For some players, putting is something you do simply to mop up a hole; for Snedeker, it's a viable way to go low.

SKILL BREAKDOWN

Pro File

Brandt Snedeker

Born December 8, 1980
Birthplace Nashville, Tenn.
Residence Nashville, Tenn.
Height / Weight 6' 1" / 185 lbs.
College Vanderbilt University
Turned professional 2004
Professional victories 7 [5 PGA Tour]*
Majors None*
Career U.S. earnings $19.6 million*

*Through 2013 U.S. Open

P utting is a tricky thing to measure. Is the best putter the guy with the least number of putts or the one with the most one-putts? It's a bit more complicated than that, really, which is why the methods used in the past for measuring putting proficiency on the PGA Tour have been enhanced by a new stat called Strokes Gained, which does a much better job of accurately showing where made putts make the biggest difference. Every time you one-putt you gain a certain number of strokes against the field, based on a carefully calculated average from that distance. You also lose strokes when you miss. Although it sounds a bit complicated, what Strokes Gained really does is rate a player's putting relative to his competitors in a tournament, which is the truest measurement of skill. Right now, the most skilled putter on Tour is Brandt Snedeker.

Great putters like Snedeker successfully match the pressure of their grip to their tempo. If you have a fast-tempo stroke but a light grip pressure, you won't be able to effectively control the putterhead as it moves through the hitting zone. If you have a slow, languid stroke but use a tight grip, you'll rob your motion of flow and feel as you swing through impact. Obviously there are endless variations in this relationship, but finding the right grip pressure for your stroke is critical to becoming a solid putter.

> "Right now, the most skilled putter on Tour is Brandt Snedeker." —Marius Filmalter

Snedeker is an excellent, decisive putter who happens to have one of the quickest tempos on Tour. Because he has a grip that's quite firm, he's able to control this fast-paced tempo and get very good results.

To figure out your own best match, go to the practice green and roll a bunch of putts. For starters, mimic the grip strength/stroke tempo combinations used by three of the best putters on Tour. If you have a fast pace, copy Brandt Snedeker and use a tighter grip (an 8 on a 10-point scale). If your tempo is neither fast nor slow, try a medium grip pressure à la Phil Mickelson (a 6), and use a loose grip like the one Luke Donald employs (a 4) if you putt with a slow tempo. Try each combination and take note of how it feels and the results you get. It shouldn't take long to determine what sort of pressure fits your technique, and when you do your results should improve dramatically.
—*Marius Filmalter, Marius Golf, Dallas, Tex.*

Rank File

PGA Tour
One-Putt Stats

Year	%	Rank
2008	39.2%	[44th]
2009	39.6%	[48th]
2010	43.9%	[2nd]
2011	42.5%	[7th]
2012	44.3%	[1st]
2013*	43.5%	[10th]

*Through May

Stats courtesy of PGATour.com

SKILL PRACTICE

Scan this photo
to watch a video of this lesson.

See the entire roll. Run that video image in your mind right before you start the putter back.

Use Your Eyes to Make More Putts

Don't just look for the line; see the putt in full

By Top 100 Teacher LOU GUZZI, Talamore C.C., Ambler, Pa.

You don't make nearly as many putts as you should, in part because you don't have a clear thought process before making your stroke. Without a clear image of the roll, you'll likely look up too early to see what the ball is doing. This leads to unwanted head movement and a halfhearted stroke that gives you little chance of making the putt. You need a new, confidence-boosting preputt method.

Instead of simply trying to see the ball go into the hole, you should try to see its entire roll (speed and line) from start to finish. Create a video of the putt in your mind, and keep that video fresh in your memory when setting up to hit your putt. Run the video just before you take the putter back and allow your stroke to respond to what you're seeing in your mind. Golf is different from other sports (e.g., baseball, football, basketball) in that you don't have your eyes on the target when you start your motion. That's why it's so important to have a clear image of what you're trying to accomplish as you stand over the ball. Create the video and then run it as you make your stroke and you'll hole a lot more putts than you do now.

QUICK TIP
If you're serious about improving, spend time practicing four- and five-footers. If you can build up your confidence on the short ones you'll feel nice and free on the longer putts.

SKILL ANALYSIS

Scan this photo to see Brandt's stroke in pure slow motion.

Head tilted to get my dominant eye (left) on the target line.

Putterface returns to neutral at impact. No adding or subtracting loft from the putter here.

WATCH & LEARN HOW I PUTT

Forget what you've learned about matching the length of your backstroke and forward-stroke and instead concentrate on your backstroke length only. I use a "pop" putting stroke, and in a pop stroke all the energy is put into the ball at impact, so your through-stroke should be basically the same every time. When I putt, the putterhead stops right after impact, and that's what you should

try to do. To vary the distance you roll the ball, experiment with different-length backstrokes (keeping your through-stroke the same) and see how far your putts travel. I let my eyes tell me how far I want the putt to travel and I just take the putterhead back as far as it needs to go. After some practice you should intuitively get the feel for your length of stroke.

The real key to the stroke, however, is impact, where you want to re-create the neutral position of the putterhead established in your setup. I never want to add or subtract loft from the putterhead at impact because either mistake can cause the ball to hop, skid or behave inconsistently some way or the other. By delivering the putterhead to the ball in a neutral position you preserve the

I hinge my wrists to swing the putter back—a major key to the pop stroke.

A short follow-through is all that's needed—all the energy went into the ball and it's gone.

Look at frame 10—you can see the clubhead has moved much more than the handle.

Scan this photo to watch a video of this lesson.

Yes!

Try This! | Hide the Puttershaft

true loft of the putter, which produces the most consistent roll time after time. I also try to strike the ball on its equator. If you're going to miss this spot, it's best to do so by hitting up on the ball a bit. It's not ideal, but it's better than hitting down on it.
—*PGA Tour player Brandt Snedeker*

Most amateurs set up to putt with their hands positioned too low and too close to the body. This creates a noticeable angle between your arms and the puttershaft, and the angle makes it difficult to hit solid putts. All you have to do is raise your hands at address

so the shaft of the putter is in line with your forearms (*photo, right*). From a down-target view, this would mean that the grip is hidden behind your right forearm, rather than protruding out as it would if your hands were lower.
—***Top 100 Teacher Mike Perpich***

STRAIGHT FROM THE SOURCE

Snedeker on Snedeker

"I've used a pop stroke on the greens for as long as I can remember, and although a lot of people call it old fashioned I think it's coming back into style. The key to the stroke is getting a bit of wrist set in the backswing and transferring all the energy into the ball at impact, not past it. Once you make contact and the ball is gone there's no reason to keep the putter moving toward the target. If you want to give the pop stroke a try, follow the keys you see here."

GRIP

I separate my hands on the grip so I can feel the club with my fingers and control the putterface with my right hand. Place the grip in the lifeline of both palms and set your left index finger over the knuckles of your right hand. Don't tie your hands together—you want them to feel the club independently.

BALL POSITION

Don't play the ball too far back in your stance. You want your putter's face to be completely neutral at address as it sits next to the ball, meaning you're not delofting (forward pressing too much) or adding loft. I have three degrees of loft on my putter, and I always make sure I'm lined up so it has its natural loft before I start my stroke.

SETUP

Check your posture by making sure that your eyes are directly over the ball. Here's an old trick you can use to practice getting it right: Hold a ball on the bridge of your nose and let it go as you stand at address. If it hits the ball on the ground, then you're solid. I also use my putter to check this position by holding it in line with your eyes and making sure it points straight down at the ball.

STATS & SPECS

When you start the putter back, do it by hinging your wrists away from the target. To get the proper feel, try my favorite drill. Place your left hand on your right bicep and hit putts with only your right hand and arm (photo, left). To do it you'll need to flex your right wrist to get enough power on the ball and you'll have to swing the clubhead more than you swing the handle of the club. Use your left hand to make sure your right elbow doesn't pop out as you make your stroke. You want to keep the right elbow down.

Snedeker vs. the Field

Snedeker's name is listed in the Top 10 of every major putting category, including the two most important to scoring: One-Putt Percentage and Strokes Gained. In 2012, he was No. 1 in both en route to his FedEx Cup title and $10 million bonus.

Stats courtesy of PGATour.com

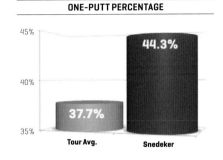

ONE-PUTT PERCENTAGE

45%

44.3%

40%

37.7%

35%

Tour Avg.   Snedeker

.86

The number of strokes Brandt Snedeker gained on the field in 2012 per round based solely on putting. This is the highest value since the stat was created in 2004.

Odyssey White Hot XG Rossie
Loft 3 degrees
Length 34 inches

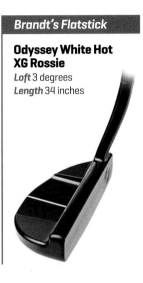

FINAL FIX

The New Way to Choose Your Putt Line

Think "track" not "line" and you'll roll smoother putts

The next time you putt, read the green and choose your line as you always do, using your regular technique. But instead of seeing your line (the path you predict the ball will take as it rolls and breaks toward the hole), picture a swath, or track. In other words, make the line you choose much wider, at least the width of the hole rather than the razor-thin strip you've been picturing.

A wider line gives you a greater margin of error, which will ease your tension at address and help you make a smoother stroke. That means better distance control, purer contact and fewer yips. Plus, a thicker line is a better representation of the real path. Your putts don't always have to hit the center of the hole to drop in—often the ones that hit the sides do just as well.

Fatten up your line and see how easy putting can be. Think of it this way: If you increased the diameter of a basketball hoop you'd make more free throws. The same principle applies when trying to hit your line.
—*Marius Filmalter*

Make your line thicker for a greater margin of error and more confidence.

Scan this photo *to watch a video of this lesson.*

LAG PUTTING

Zach
Johnson

Zach Johnson has averaged less than one three-putt a round for his entire professional career, playing on the most difficult greens on the planet. Compare that with most amateurs, who often leave a makeable putt six feet short. Zach's smart—he knows the goal isn't to make 40-footers. The key to scoring is limiting the number of strokes taken on the green to two, regardless of how far you are from the pin.

Armed with the same flatstick for more than a decade, Zach Johnson is a model of putting consistency, especially from long range.

SKILL BREAKDOWN

"Good lag putters such as Zach Johnson never allow tension to manipulate their stroke."—Marius Filmalter

The anxiety you feel standing over a makeable 4-foot putt is understandable—the pressure to score can be almost too much to bear at times. Anxiety standing over a 40-footer, however, makes zero sense, especially when the goal on any lag putt is simply to roll the ball close enough for a ho-hum two putt. Yet amateurs freeze up on lags as much as they do on knee-knockers. The tension is enough to cause the putter to decelerate at impact, leaving the putt way short, or speed it up and knock what was supposed to be an easy lag 10 feet past. Good lag putters such as Zach Johnson never allow tension to manipulate their stroke. They remain calm and confident on putts of all lengths.

The best way to alleviate tension when you putt is actually a simple one: smooth out your tempo. One of the most common mistakes I see amateurs make is a jab stroke that goes back slowly and then jerks forward into the ball in a sudden burst. You might not feel it in your motion, but trust me: it's there. Smoothing out the overall pace of your stroke eliminates jabbing as if by magic and, more important, starts to give you confidence in your technique.

Here's a drill I actually learned from one of the best putters of his generation, Brad Faxon. The next time you go to the practice green, try humming or whistling during your backstroke and forward-stroke. The tune should be "one-two," like a metronome. Your goal is to match the movement of your stroke to the rhythm of the tune so that it takes on a steady, smooth tempo. Don't try to "hit" the ball. Instead, feel like your putter is floating backward and then forward at the same smooth rate.

—*Marius Filmalter, Marius Golf, Dallas, Tex.*

SKILL PRACTICE

How to Get a Feel for Lag Putts

Trust your hands, not your eyes

Don't track the result of your putt with your eyes. Track it with feel.

By Top 100 Teacher **CHARLIE KING**, *Reynolds Plantation Golf Academy, Greensboro, Ga.*

You inevitably gain a ton of strokes thanks to three-putts or poor putting in general. You closely monitor the result of every putt by watching where the ball goes, but you don't do anything to tie the result to the feel of your stroke. If you want to improve your putting, you need to know what good and bad strokes feel like.

The best way to get to know how your stroke should feel is to putt without watching the ball as it rolls. By keeping your head down, you'll concentrate on the motion and not on the result and you'll be much more aware of the type of stroke you're making.

A great drill is to take three balls and hit lag putts on a practice green. Keep your head down and grade each putt—short, long, missed to the left, etc. After a few seconds, look up to see if the grade you assigned the putt while you were looking down at the ground matches the result. If it doesn't, adjust your stroke on the next putt, and keep rolling balls until your grades consistently match the actual roll. Repeat this drill often enough and your feel for distance will jump off the charts.

SKILL ANALYSIS

WATCH & LEARN THE SKINNY ON LAG TECHNIQUE

From long distance, you try to swing your putter along the target line, in a straight-back-and-straight-through path. This often causes you to take the club to the outside on the backstroke and almost always prevents you from properly releasing the putterhead through impact. The result is putts that are blocked and sliced—and very few balls rolling into the hole, especially from long range. Good lag putters do the opposite—and you should too. Your key will be to open a "window" between your arms in your backstroke and then shut it as you move through impact. To do this, follow the steps on these pages.

—*Top 100 Teacher Jim Hardy, Plane Truth Golf, Houston, Tex.*

ADDRESS

Take your address position and make certain that your arms are parallel to each other so that if you were looking in a mirror to your right, your right arm would hide your left.

BACKSTROKE

Take the club away by gently pulling your right elbow to the inside. It should move at about a 45-degree angle to your target line. If you were to look in a mirror you'd see a "window" open between your arms.

Scan this photo
to watch a video of this lesson.

STATS & SPECS

Zach vs. the Field

While even the most confident pro won't give himself much of a chance from greater than 25 feet, these putts can and do go in, and Zach Johnson's long putts tend to drop more often than the PGA Tour average.

MAKE PERCENTAGE FROM > 25 FEET

Tour Avg.: **5.1%**
Johnson: **8.0%**

Stats from 2012 season; courtesy of PGATour.com

Zach's Flatstick

SeeMore FGP Black

In Johnson's bag since 2003 (the year he won Player of the Year honors on the Web.com Tour), the FGP has helped Johnson win nine PGA Tour titles, including the 2007 Masters.

FINAL FIX

Lag with Your Big Muscles

The secret to rolling the ball straight and the right distance is in your core

The key to solving your putting woes from long distance is to control the putter with the muscles in your core instead of your hands and arms. Here's how to do it:

Step 1 Hold your putter out in front of your body so it's parallel to the ground. Make sure you hold it with your normal putting grip.

Step 2 Rotate your body to your right in a mock backstroke. Use only your core. Your right shoulder should move slightly behind you.

Step 3 Now rotate your body in the opposite direction so your arms and putter are pulled through the impact area and into a finish position left of your left hip.

Continue to rotate back and forth using only your abs to power the club left and right. If you do it correctly your core will tire after a few minutes. The more you remove hand and arm action from your stroke, the better.

—*Marius Filmalter*

Scan this photo *to watch a video of this lesson.*

Start here...

...engage your core and turn to here...

...and then all the way to your finish.

FORWARD-STROKE

Straighten your right elbow so that, at impact, it's in the same position it held at address. Then, swing forward by letting your left elbow pull in a bit, as your right did in the backswing. This will again open a "window" between your arms and naturally release the putterhead.

QUICK TIP
Take the same stance width so that you can accurately monitor the length of your strokes—right foot for your backstrokes, left foot for your through-strokes. This makes it easy to control speed.

Skill No. 17
STROKE CONSISTENCY

Jason
Day

Avoiding three-putts is a legitimate way to keep your scores down. So is sinking putts on your first attempt. Jason Day combines a deft green-reading eye, a knack for visualizing the line and a rock-solid stroke to hole putts other players on the PGA Tour merely get close.

Speed and distance control are critical to sinking putts, and Jason Day has exceptional command of both.

SKILL BREAKDOWN

Scan this photo *to watch a video of this lesson.*

"One of the reasons Jason Day is so good at making putts on the first attempt is that he knows how to roll the ball at the right speed and the right distance on every putt." —Marius Filmalter

One of the reasons Jason Day is so good at making putts on the first attempt is that he knows how to roll the ball at the right speed and the right distance on every putt. If you need help in either of these areas, give the following drill a try. It's a quick and easy way to build an inventory of stroke lengths that will allow you to putt the ball three distinct distances.

Step 1 Roll It 40 Feet
Hit the practice green with a small bucket of balls. Get into your regular stance, and roll a few putts by taking your hands back to just outside your right thigh and then motoring through at your best putting-stroke pace. Notice how this stroke rolls the ball about 40 feet. (You may roll it longer or shorter depending on your stance width and tempo.)

Step 2 Roll It 20 Feet
Roll a few more, but this time stop your hands when they reach the middle of your right thigh in your backstroke. **Make sure your stance width is the same as the one you used for the first round of putts and that you apply the same pace and force to your stroke.** This stroke should roll the ball about 20 feet.

Step 3 Roll It 10 Feet
Repeat the drill, but this time stop your stroke when your hands swing back to the inside of your right thigh. Again, use the same stance width and tempo. If you did it correctly, these should roll about 10 feet.

Voilà! Three defined strokes that you can count on to roll the ball three common distances, which is probably three more than you have right now!
—*Marius Filmalter, Marius Golf, Dallas, Tex.*

SKILL PRACTICE

Make Short Putts Automatic

This drill does the trick every time

Scan this photo to watch a video of this lesson.

Yes!

You need to consciously practice stroking your putter straight over your line on short putts.

No!

More than 70 percent of golfers unwittingly pull the putterhead to the left.

By Top 100 Teacher KEITH LYFORD, Old Greenwood G.C., Truckee, Calif.

You tend to lose an inordinate number of strokes per round because you're just not solid on short putts. You're not alone—my research shows that about 75 percent of all recreational golfers cut across the target line with the putter, which can result in both pulls and pushes.

Here's how to remedy the situation. Find a flat area around a hole on the practice green and line up about a foot away from the hole without a ball. Now make a few practice strokes and watch where your putterhead goes in relation to the hole. What you will probably find is that the head of your putter doesn't cross the center of the hole but actually moves to the left side of it [*inset photo*]. This is a cut stroke, and it will never produce consistent results.

Now make a practice stroke in which the head of your putter goes directly over the center of the hole [*main photo*]. This move will probably feel quite a bit different from your normal stroke, but it's what you need to do if you want to be a consistent short putter. Make about a dozen strokes like this, each time making sure that your putterhead passes directly over the hole. Once this stroke feels comfortable, take a ball and try to do the same thing. You should find that it rolls directly into the middle of the hole—just like it's supposed to.

SKILL ANALYSIS

WATCH & LEARN SINK PUTTS WITH YOUR ELBOW

My access to computer-generated data on 50,000 putting strokes puts me in a unique position: I know what good putters do and what bad putters don't do. Part of any kind of putting analysis is looking at techniques that generate the best results, and for my money you can't beat the one used by Jack Nicklaus, a player who always seemed to make his best strokes when he needed them most.

There are a lot of good things to copy in Nicklaus's putting stroke, but none are more important than the position of his right elbow, which was always tucked against the right side of his torso from start to finish. This right-elbow position—something I see in the stroke of current PGA Tour star Jason Day—is a key component in swinging your putter back and through on the correct path and with good tempo.

Unfortunately, I see a lot of amateurs trying to power their strokes with their arms. This invariably causes them to move their right elbow out and away. **The problem is, when you lose your right elbow/torso connection, the putter rises up off the ground, making it difficult to strike the ball squarely.** Elbow separation also occurs if you try to take the putter straight back and through. There's no way you can trace a straight line with your putterhead without losing your right-arm connection on your backstroke and your left-elbow connection on your through-stroke.
—*Marius Filmalter, Marius Golf, Dallas, Tex.*

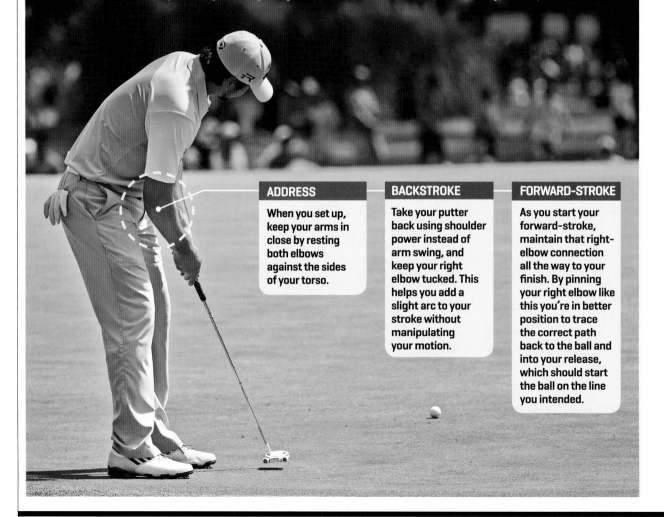

ADDRESS

When you set up, keep your arms in close by resting both elbows against the sides of your torso.

BACKSTROKE

Take your putter back using shoulder power instead of arm swing, and keep your right elbow tucked. This helps you add a slight arc to your stroke without manipulating your motion.

FORWARD-STROKE

As you start your forward-stroke, maintain that right-elbow connection all the way to your finish. By pinning your right elbow like this you're in better position to trace the correct path back to the ball and into your release, which should start the ball on the line you intended.

TRY THIS DRILL

Pin your right biceps against the right side of your chest using your left hand as a vise, then putt with your right hand only. As you hit putts like this, you'll start to feel how the connection forces you to use your shoulders to swing the putter instead of your arms and how the putterhead traces a nice arc both back and through. It helps to think of finishing your putt with your right shoulder closer to your chin than it was at address.

STATS & SPECS

Day vs. the Field

There are literally dozens of stats to help determine who has the hot flatstick on Tour, and a good one to look at is One-Putt-Percentage. This stat tells you who has the ability to get the ball in the hole without wasting another stroke, whether the stroke is made following a green hit in regulation or a chip or pitch after missing the green altogether. Day's percentage, despite his youth, is well above the PGA Tour average.

ONE-PUTT PERCENTAGE

45%

40%

35%

37.7% Tour Avg.

42.6% Day

Stats from 2012 season; courtesy of PGATour.com

Day's Putter

TaylorMade Ghost Spider S
Loft 3 degrees
Length 34 inches

FINAL FIX

Perfect Putts In Five Steps

This "freeze-fixing" preputt routine has been a hit on Tour

You're facing a tricky 6-footer and you just can't seem...to...pull...the...trigger. You freeze—a putting malady that takes you out of your natural rhythm and makes executing a smooth stroke impossible. If this sounds like you, copy what many great putters do. Confident golfers typically step in, spread their feet, look at the hole, then the ball, and then putts I suggest you set up and then count the steps in your head as you execute them. When you first look down,

count "1." Count "2" as you look back to the ball, and so on (*photos below*). Build some tempo into this cycle. You should complete each step in rhythmic time (i.e., don't jump from one step to the next faster or slower than you do for the others). The five-frame cycle is ideal. Anything less than that and you're probably not giving the putt your best effort; anything longer than 5 is treading toward "freeze" territory.

—*Marius Filmalter*

QUICK TIP
Take your normal address, but turn each toe in toward the middle of your stance, like you're pigeon-toed. This restricts excess movement by limiting the flexibility in your lower body.

COUNT "1" Step in.

COUNT "2" Take your stance.

COUNT "3" Look at your target.

COUNT "4" Look back at the ball.

"5" Pull the trigger!

You have a swing, but it's the sum of several important and distinct parts. And while it's a good idea to think of your swing as a single, fluid motion, breaking it down and working on it in pieces is the Tour way to ensure that everything is firing on all cylinders. Our all-star cast of Tour pros in this section have won a combined 22 majors. Copy their swings position-by-position to eliminate common mistakes in your address, backswing, transition, downswing and so on. What you'll find is that improving one section of your motion automatically improves the sections that come before and after it. For the final touches, we enlist the greatest player of this or any generation, Tiger Woods, to combine all of those working parts into a powerful, flowing thing of beauty.

To use the Scan-It/See-It feature in this section, look for the SCAN boxes (*example at right*). For instructions, see page 9. Videos also available at golf.com/plap.

Scan this photo to access bonus videos and lessons.

HOW TO PLAY LIKE...

- **Louis Oosthuizen**
  Get his address

- **Ian Poulter**
  Follow his backswing

- **Rickie Fowler**
  Steal his transition

- **Rory McIlroy**
  Get his impact position

- **Ernie Els**
  Repeat his tempo

- **Adam Scott**
  Get his all-around swing

- **Tiger Woods**
  Copy everything!

PLAY LIKE A PRO

SECTION 4

FULL SWING

ESSENTIALS

Louis
Oosthuizen

The 2010 British Open champion and 2012 Masters runner-up does so many things well in his driver and iron swings that it's impossible to list them all. What can be listed are all of the great things he does in his setup position that make what comes after even better. An address like Oosthuizen's—one of the best in the game—stops swing errors before they can start.

Just about every part of Louis Oosthuizen's technique is perfect, but his address position is exceptional. Copy him or pay the price.

SKILL BREAKDOWN

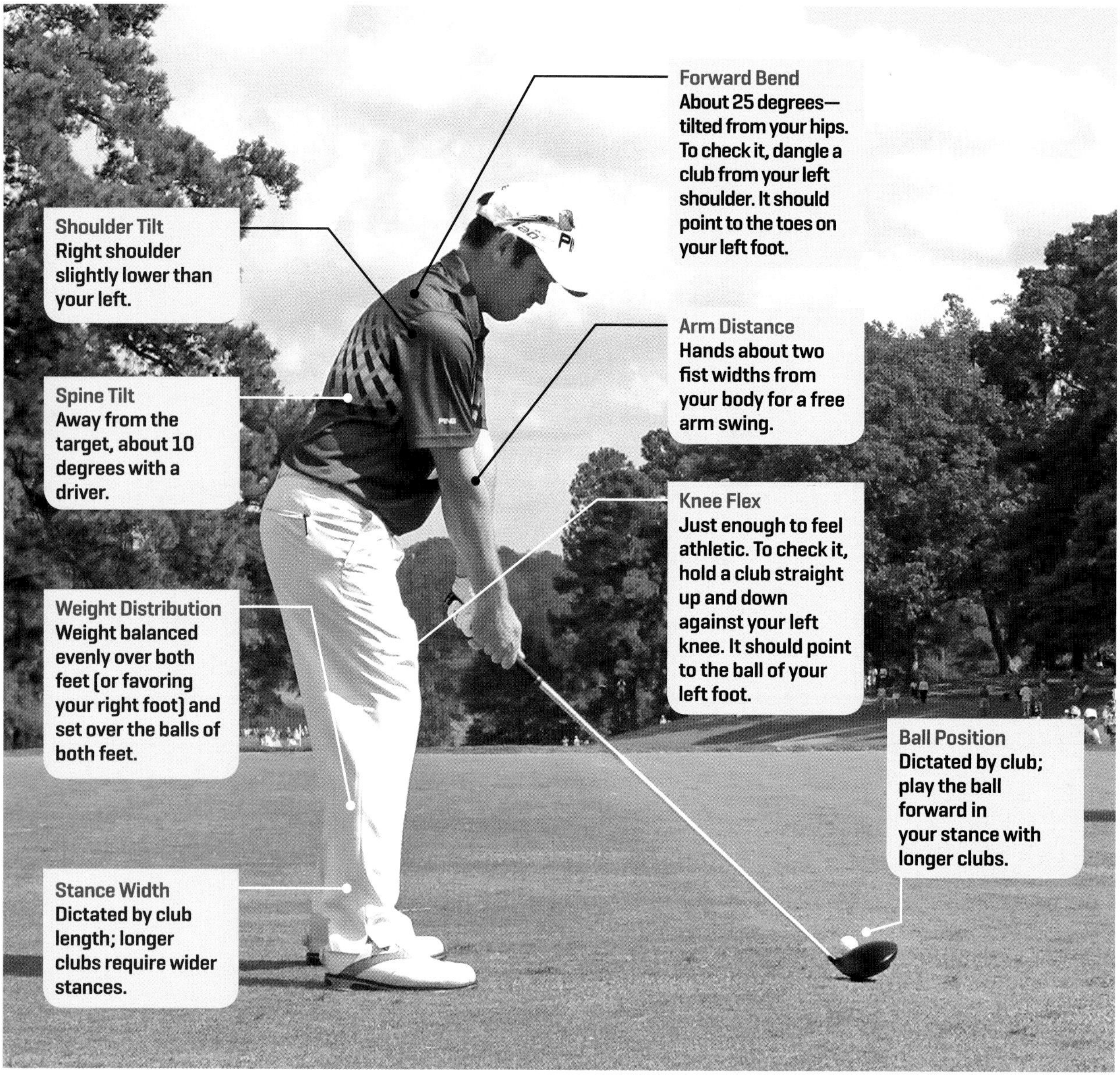

Forward Bend
About 25 degrees—tilted from your hips. To check it, dangle a club from your left shoulder. It should point to the toes on your left foot.

Shoulder Tilt
Right shoulder slightly lower than your left.

Arm Distance
Hands about two fist widths from your body for a free arm swing.

Spine Tilt
Away from the target, about 10 degrees with a driver.

Knee Flex
Just enough to feel athletic. To check it, hold a club straight up and down against your left knee. It should point to the ball of your left foot.

Weight Distribution
Weight balanced evenly over both feet (or favoring your right foot) and set over the balls of both feet.

Ball Position
Dictated by club; play the ball forward in your stance with longer clubs.

Stance Width
Dictated by club length; longer clubs require wider stances.

The way you stand over the ball defines the structure of your swing as well as its chance for failure or success. The picture above shows how to get into a fundamentally correct address position consistently and without error, using one of the best in the game—Louis Oosthuizen—as an example.

When working on your address position, do it in front of a full-length mirror and copy the positions that you see on this page and on the ones that follow. As the saying goes, a picture is worth a thousand words. Take in what your body feels like, but remember: this is only a guide. There have been thousands of great players over the years, and no two setups have ever been perfect matches. That having been said, sticking to the time-proven fundamentals that go into Oosthuizen's setup will get you in position to start your swing on plane and increase your chances of hitting a successful shot.
—*Top 100 Teacher Lou Guzzi, Talamore C.C., Ambler, Pa.*

SKILL PRACTICE

No!
If you stand too far away from the ball with your upper body hunched over...

No!
...your right arm will swing inside the handle when you allow it to hang.

Yes!
When you stand the correct distance from the ball with good posture...

Yes!
...your right arm won't change position (relative to the handle) when you allow it to hang.

Set Your Stance for a Better Swing Plane

Standing too far from the ball robs you of speed and accuracy—plus a lot of new golf balls

By Top 100 Teacher MARK HACKETT, Old Palm G.C., Palm Beach Gardens, Fla.

Before you start rebuilding your entire motion to fix your plane problems, take a look at your address position and, specifically, how far you're standing from the ball. If you're too far away (a very common mistake among amateurs, especially with the driver), the shaft of your driver will be too flat and you'll feel the need to hunch over more at address. Bending over too far automatically sets you up to swing too steep, both going back and coming down.

An easy way to check if you're standing the correct distance from the ball is to simply take your address position, remove your right hand from the handle and allow your right arm to hang. If you're too far away from the ball, your right arm and hand will settle somewhere between your body and the handle (*top photos*). Basically, the perfect distance from the ball—combined with the right amount of forward bend—is the one that allows your arms to dangle straight down from your shoulder sockets (*bottom photos*). From this position you're set up to swing the club on the correct plane and plug the power leaks that come from falling off plane at the very start. You'll see extra yards the next time you play.

SKILL ANALYSIS

Scan this photo to see Louis's swing in pure slow motion.

Perfectly square setup with the right arm hiding the left from this angle.

Because his setup is so good, Oosthuizen can turn everything at the same time and at the same pace.

Balance at setup leads to balance during the swing. No lifting or dropping here.

Both hands above his head, level and parallel with the club. Perfect!

Still in balance and still in his address posture this deep into his downswing. Copy this.

As good an impact position as you'll find, with the left arm on the chest and right arm on the right hip. Hands are a near mirror image of address.

WATCH & LEARN SET UP FOR SUCCESS

Louis Oosthuizen has one of the most beautiful and simplest swings on earth, so it wasn't a surprise that he came within an eyelash of winning his second major at the 2012 Masters. I think his setup has a lot to do with how effortlessly he swings the club. Over the ball, Oosthuizen is so athletic that he looks like he could excel in almost any sport. He could be ready to shoot a free throw, return a serve or belt a home run. **Take special note of the tilt in his spine and how he extends his forearms and maintains a sizable width between his knees—these are great ways to put a solid driver swing in motion.**

During his swing, Oosthuizen keeps his lower body stable and balanced while pivoting his upper body extensively back and through. This is a great lesson for amateurs, who often use too much lower-body action and not enough upper-body turn. Another key is how he pushes the club away from the ball using his forearms and then again when he reaches the top. Try these two moves and see if you don't increase your leverage and power.
—*Top 100 Teacher Dana Rader, Ballantyne Resort, Charlotte, N.C.*

FINAL FIX

How to Fix a Faulty Setup

A magazine is all you need

By Top 100 Teacher **CAROL PREISINGER**, *The Kiawah Island Club, Kiawah Island, S.C.*

It happens every time you address the ball: You're not sure how far apart your feet should be, where to position your hands or where to play the ball in your stance. As a result, your swing and your shots are inconsistent to the point that you have no idea where the ball is going from one round to the next.

To fix this problem, lay a magazine (may I suggest *Golf Magazine*?) on the ground with the covers face up and follow the checkpoints at right.

1 Align the insteps on both feet with the edges of the magazine.
2 Ball and hands aligned to the magazine's spine (where the pages are glued together).
3 Eyes over the top edge of the magazine.
4 Hands over the bottom edge of the magazine.

Pro File

Louis Oosthuizen

Full name Lodewicus Theodorus Oosthuizen
Born October 19, 1982
Birthplace Mossel Bay, South Africa
Residence Pinnacle Point, South Africa
Height / Weight 5' 10" / 170 lbs.
College None
Turned professional 2002
Professional victories 11 (1 PGA Tour)*
Majors 2010 British Open*
Career U.S. earnings $5.9 million*

*Through 2013 U.S. Open

Rank File

PGA Tour Stats

Driving Distance	**299.5 yds.** (23rd)
Clubhead Speed	**116.8 mph** (43rd)
Driving Accuracy	**62.4%** (67th)
Greens in Regulation	**68.8%** (15th)

2012 season; courtesy of PGATour.com

Louis's Driver

PING Anser

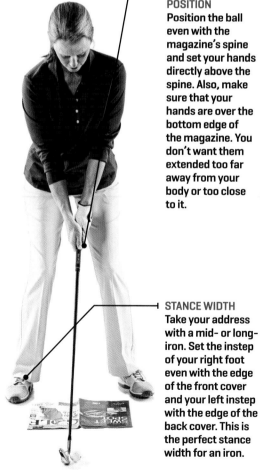

HAND/BALL POSITION
Position the ball even with the magazine's spine and set your hands directly above the spine. Also, make sure that your hands are over the bottom edge of the magazine. You don't want them extended too far away from your body or too close to it.

STANCE WIDTH
Take your address with a mid- or long-iron. Set the instep of your right foot even with the edge of the front cover and your left instep with the edge of the back cover. This is the perfect stance width for an iron.

POSTURE
Bend from your hips, keeping your back nice and flat until your eyes are over the top edge of the magazine. You don't want your head too far out in front of your toes, nor do you want to address the ball while standing too erect.

Skill No. 19
BACKSWING

Ian
Poulter

The Ryder Cup star hits fairways and greens at a very high percentage. One reason is that he sets up a compensation-free downswing by getting the club in great position at the top. His textbook backswing is a great one for amateurs to copy, not only for its simplicity, but also because the No. 12 ranked player in the world has proved that it works.

There's more to Ian Poulter's game than Ryder Cup fist-pumps, including a perfectly simple backswing that gets everything right at the top.

SKILL BREAKDOWN

Scan this photo for a one-on-one lesson with Ian Poulter.

Fold Time
Start folding your right elbow as soon as you start turning your buckle and buttons. Fold it using a smooth motion, as if you're bringing a soda can to your lips (not as if you're starting a lawn mower).

Connected
A unified turn keeps your address posture—and swing center—intact and the clubhead outside your hands at this point in the backswing.

Simple Turn
Shirt buttons and belt buckle turning together and at the same speed.

Make an "L"
If you turn as you fold, your forearms will rotate smoothly to the right and set the clubshaft and clubface on plane. Do it correctly and The clubshaft and your left arm form a capital "L" with your left wrist fully hinged.

Good backswings such as Ian Poulter's don't feature many moving parts or a lot of arm and hand action. If you feel a little out of control as you start the club back, focus on two points: 1) your belt buckle and 2) the buttons on your shirt. **Begin your motion by turning the buckle and the buttons to the right at the same time and at the same speed without losing your posture.** Allow your arms and the club to move with your body turn.

Notice that by turning your belt buckle and buttons you're automatically turning your hips and shoulders. Because each side of your hips, and both shoulders, can work independently of each other, focusing on your buckle and buttons pulls everything together and makes it easier to repeat this move successfully under pressure.

The only move you're required to make with your arms as you turn back is to fold your right elbow.
—*Top 100 Teacher Mike Perpich, RiverPines G.C., Johns Creek, Ga.*

SKILL PRACTICE

Scan this photo *to watch a video of this lesson.*

Hold a club upside down using your left hand only.

Swing your left arm back while turning your shoulders.

Set your right hand on the club. Instant perfect top position.

Find Your Natural Backswing

Swing with your left arm only to groove your best move back

By Top 100 Teacher RICK McCORD, *The McCord Golf Academy at Orange Lake G.C., Orlando, Fla.*

You consistently put yourself in a bad position at the top of your backswing because you lift the club up or whip it way to the inside. Either error makes it almost impossible to swing back down on plane. You're doing this because, like most golfers, you're trying to hit certain positions when you swing. Fighting your natural tendencies like this makes it difficult to get your body in a balanced position that supports the club at the top.

To fix your backswing issues and find your perfect top position, follow the steps at right.

Step 1 Turn your 6-iron around so the grip is facing the ground (it'll be lighter and easier to swing this way) and grip the club in your left hand only.

Step 2 This one is easy—swing the club back while turning your shoulders. Feel how using just your left arm gets you away from

"position" golf and allows you to make a smoother move to the top.

Step 3 Place your right hand on the club—this is the position your body naturally wants to take at the top. As if by magic you've nailed all the requirements for a solid backswing. Trust it and use it.

SKILL ANALYSIS

Scan this photo to see Poults's swing in pure slow motion.

An upright setup and takeaway (high chest and hands), but with his weight balanced from heel to toe.

Clubhead aligned with the target line and clubface parallel to the spine.

Right elbow folds earlier than most, but club on plane and moving up nicely.

Shaft pointing at the ball and passing through the right shoulder. Perfect.

Arm swing lifts the club from the shaft plane to the shoulder plane. Every golfer does this. The trick is to get it back on plane prior to impact.

The club looks laid off, but it's consistent with his less-than-full body turn. Poulter turns back only as far as his body allows him to.

WATCH & LEARN BACKSWING BASICS

In an age when almost everyone knocks it 300 yards, Ian Poulter chooses to rely on accuracy, course-management skills and a world-class short game. (He led the PGA Tour in Scrambling in 2012.) His style is as old-school as his tartan pants. Poulter also ranks high in final-round scoring (70.4 in 2012), which tells you something about his spirit, tenacity and will to win.

On the tee box, Poulter makes two backswing moves that every amateur should pay attention to. The first is when he traces a wide swing arc, which allows him to switch to a narrow approach on the way down. (You can't have it both ways.) The second is how **he stops his shoulder turn when his body can no longer rotate.** Swinging beyond this range is a recipe for disaster. Poulter has

said that he likes to focus on keeping the clubhead low to the ground and swinging it back to the inside using only his shoulders. Following his advice will certainly increase the likelihood that you'll approach the ball from inside the target line instead of swiping it at like you do when you swing over the top.
—*Terry Rowles, San Francisco Golf Performance Center, San Francisco, Calif.*

FINAL FIX

The Magic Backswing Move for Straight Shots

Keep your elbows down to bust your slice

By Top 100 Teacher KELLIE STENZEL,
Palm Beach G.C., Palm Beach, Fla.

There are a number of errors you can make that will lead to a chronic slice, but the biggest and most prevalent one is an open clubface at impact. Regardless of your swing shape or plane, if you don't get the clubface square, you won't be able to hit the ball straight or with any right-to-left movement.

My guess is that you're leaving the clubface open, because 1] you have a faulty grip and 2] your arms don't function properly during your swing. Check your right elbow. Chances are it's flying open in your backswing, meaning

the back of your right elbow points behind you rather than at the ground as you move to the top. This makes it very difficult to control the clubface and typically leads to an open position at impact. Same goes for your left elbow—it, too, needs to point at the ground, but this time on the target side of your swing. Many slicers are forced into a "chicken-wing" position in the release, meaning that the left elbow is bent sharply and pointing behind the body.

The next time you visit the range, start your session by making half-speed swings and focusing on pointing your right elbow down in your backswing and your left elbow down after. Think "elbows down" from start to finish and you'll be well on your way to straighter shots.

At the top, elbows point to the ground.

In the finish, elbows still point to the ground.

QUICK TIP
Start your backswing with a simple move: Swing your left elbow back along the target line. It's an easy way to get everything moving correctly at the start.

Skill No. 20
TRANSITION

Rickie
Fowler

With one of the quickest swings on Tour, Rickie Fowler transitions so fast from backswing to downswing that if you blink you'll miss it. This isn't to say he's reckless, because the fundamentals are all there, and his lightning-quick change of direction at the top is what actually slots the club on the perfect plane.

Rickie Fowler's lightening-quick transition and even faster all-around tempo serve not only to create speed, but to slot the club perfectly on plane.

STRAIGHT FROM THE SOURCE

By whipping my hips into action the moment I complete my backswing...

...the clubshaft bisects my right forearm, and the clubhead moves to the ball from the inside. Perfect.

The transition from backswing to downswing is where amateurs make the most mistakes, usually because they're thinking about what to do instead of just doing it. My move at the top is simple, so it's easy to repeat without having to think about it.

I use my shoulders on my backswing to power the club back. Once I get to the top, however, my lower body takes over.

Notice how my belt buckle is clearly visible in the left photo above, but you can't see it in the right photo. I've turned hard with my hips and tried to leave everything else behind.

When I start my downswing with my hips, notice how I automatically create separation between my upper and lower body. In the left photo my shoulders are more rotated than my hips, and in the right photo my hips

are more rotated than my shoulders. This is the true source of power in any swing. Also notice how my driver shaft has responded to the separation by dropping down and onto what most golf experts would call the ideal plane with the clubface rotating to square. This is what makes any swing ultra-accurate. I accomplished all of this by simply turning my lower body. Easy.
—*PGA Tour Player Rickie Fowler*

SKILL PRACTICE

Scan this photo to watch a video of this lesson.

Before you reach shoulder height...

...start turning your lower body back to the ball...

...and add lag and tons of swing power.

How to Snap It Down from the Top

Stay in control and drive it longer at the same time

By Top 100 Teacher BRADY RIGGS, Woodley Lakes G.C., Van Nuys, Calif.

In an effort to hit your longest shots you make a backswing that's way too long. Not only does this mistake actually sap your power by forcing your swing out of sequence, it also has a negative effect on the quality of your ballstriking and accuracy. Basically,

overswinging is a huge error. You need to shorten your backswing, or at least that's how it should feel. The key to driving the ball with power is to deliver the club back to the ball squarely, and a shorter backswing will help you make solid contact and swing in sequence so that your arms and body are synchronized. The ball doesn't care how long your backswing is when you

catch it in the center of the face—it's going to go far. To tighten up your swing and accomplish both of these keys, follow these steps:

Step 1 Make your backswing as you normally would, but don't allow your hands to go past shoulder height.

Step 2 Start turning your hips back toward the ball before you feel like your

"normal" backswing is complete.

Step 3 You should feel a "whip" in your swing, which will create more speed.

QUICK TIP

If you unwind your hips correctly it should feel like your back is facing the target (as it does at the end of your backswing) even after you start turning your hips.

SKILL ANALYSIS

Scan this photo to see Rickie's swing in pure slow motion.

1. Clubhead starts back while tracking outside the hands. Whipping the club to the inside is a death move.

2. Left arm swings across the chest with the hands in close to the body.

3. Folding the right elbow sets the club on the shoulder plane.

4. Right elbow drops and slots the club.

5. Hips open up while the shoulders remain closed. This is perfect.

6. Power delivery: left arm on chest and right elbow in front of right hip. This is as good as a pre-impact position can get.

WATCH & LEARN GET FLAT AND FAST

Rickie Fowler's swing reminds me a lot of Sergio García's. El Niño continues to be one of the best ballstrikers on Tour, and he always hits it solidly. The same is true of Fowler. For a guy who weighs only 150 pounds, Rickie kills it. But there's more to Fowler than power. He controls trajectory and shot shape better than anyone, which is amazing for a golfer his age. He swings fast, but can produce draws, fades, low shots and high shots without blinking an eye.

Rickie's natural swing plane is a bit lower than what you see with most players, yet his technique is well worth copying. **As soon as he reaches the top, he clears his left side from the ground up and with such speed that his club drops from his shoulder plane all the way down to the shaft plane.** You can tell that this is his natural track to the ball by the way he maintains his spine angle and distance from the ball. Mechanics aside, Fowler plays with a take-no-prisoners attitude. He's humble, but he has zero doubts about his ability and believes that he's as good as anyone on Tour.
—*Top 100 Teacher Mike Adams, The Medalist Club, Hobe Sound, Fla., and Hamilton Farm G.C., Gladstone, N.J.*

FINAL FIX

Add Yards with Your Transition

Try my step drill to fix your weight shift and gain power

By Top 100 Teacher RON GRING,
Magnolia Grove G.C., Mobile, Ala.

The drill below is an easy way to ingrain the feeling of a proper transition so you can pick up big yards quickly.

Step 1 Set up with your weight distributed equally between both feet.

Step 2 Swing back, feeling as though you're pushing off your left foot.

Step 3 Allow your left foot to come off the ground and move a few inches closer to your right foot, as if you're trying to click your heels together. You should be fully loaded on your right leg by the time your hands reach waist height.

Step 4 Just before you transition to your downswing, drive off the inside of your right foot and then step in and plant your left foot ahead of the ball—this should all happen as you end your backswing. If you've ever played baseball, this should feel as though you're stepping into a pitch. Once you plant, the key is to swing aggressively through the ball. You should feel a whiplike sensation as you transition to your downswing, which will create much more leverage—and speed—at impact.

Scan this photo to watch a video of this lesson.

Exaggerate your weight shift going back...

...then shift aggressively forward before you end your backswing to max out your downswing sequence and speed.

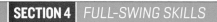

Skill No. 21
IMPACT

Rory
McIlroy

Here's all you need to know about Rory McIlroy's freakish power: He has faster hips than any golfer ever studied and about twice as fast as the average weekend player. This allows him to generate more power pound-for-pound than any golfer on Tour.

Rory McIlroy's swing is certainly otherworldly, but anyone can copy his downswing basics to add power at impact and compress the ball for max yards.

SKILL BREAKDOWN

QUICK TIP
The simple way to a more dynamic impact? Swing for the fences. Loosen up your arms, wrists and hands and let them swing freely and quickly—almost furiously—in your practice swing with zero tension.

BALANCE
Rory uses his body as a support mechanism to stay in balance, even when topping 120 mph on the swingspeed meter.

CRACK THE WHIP
Whether he's hitting driver or an iron, Rory "cracks the whip" with a perfect downswing sequence that saves all his energy for impact.

PERFECT POSITION
Hips wide open and shoulders slightly closed.

That sound you hear when a whip is cracked is caused by the incredible speed of the whip's end as it unleashes all of its built-up energy. This phenomenon is very similar to the way Rory McIlroy unleashes the power of his swing into the ball. If you've noticed, Rory isn't a huge guy, but he winds up his body on the way back and then swings in sequence on the way down with his hips rotating at full blast,

and then—just like the handle of a bullwhip—stopping for a split second just before impact. **This move unloads all of the power he has built up in his arms and hands to the clubhead and, ultimately, the ball.**

To ingrain the feeling of cracking the whip like Rory, hold a ball in the fingers of your right hand. Set up just as you would to hit a shot (with a ball on the ground in front of you), take your right hand to the top as you would in your

normal swing, then simply try to throw the ball in your hand directly at the ball on the ground. After a few tries, you'll notice that you have to hold the ball loosely in order to hit the ball on the ground without releasing it too soon. Repeat this move until you can do it consistently, then pick up a club and feel like you're throwing the clubhead at the ball with the same feel as in the drill.
—*Top 100 Teacher Peter Kostis, Kostis-McCord Learning Center, Scottsdale, Ariz.*

SKILL PRACTICE

Make a Stronger Impact with the Right Pivot

The right turn gives you more yards with less effort

By Top 100 Teacher **CHRIS COMO**,
Gleneagles C.C., Plano, Tex.

You try to move the club with your hands and arms but fail to support this movement with your body. Not only is this a very weak way to deliver the club to the ball, it also tends to create slices that sap even more distance out of your shots.

To properly support your hands and arms and create more power with your body, you need to rotate your hips in addition to moving them laterally when you swing down and through the ball. You've probably only tried to either rotate or move laterally, but you need to do both in order to pivot correctly.

In the corner of a room, take your address position without a club and fold your arms across your chest. Set up with one wall to your left and another directly behind you. As you turn through in a mock downswing, keep your left hip on the wall behind you (the rotation part of correct hip action) while thrusting your belt buckle toward the wall to your left (the lateral part) without losing your address posture. This is how good players pivot, and it's key to supporting your upper body through the swing while creating significantly more swing power.

Rotate while keeping your left hip on the wall behind you...

...and shift toward the target so your belt buckle faces the wall on your left.

SKILL ANALYSIS

Scan this photo
to see Rory's swing
in pure slow motion.

Check the creases above his pants pockets. Rory has crouched as well as turned on his way to the top.

This is the key to Rory's power: His hips explode out of the gate and separate from the rest of his body like the first booster on a rocket.

Still in his crouch, the massive hip unwind creates a slingshot effect that propels Rory's torso, arms and club into action.

As the hips eventually slow down, the shoulders and arms pick up the pace.

Compare this picture with frame 6. It's all hand speed as energy runs from his body through his hands to the clubhead.

Rory's hips have gone from 49 degrees closed at the top to 62 degrees open at impact. (The Tour average is 30 to 48 degrees open at impact.)

WATCH & LEARN FIRE AT THE RIGHT TARGET

When amateurs release their hips on their downswing—if at all—they tend to thrust straight out toward the ball or simply turn them in place. These moves are big-time no-nos. **Great players such as Rory McIlroy release their hips on their downswing by firing them to the right of the target and then halting this action until momentum drags the hips to the left of the target.** Again, this gives the appearance that good players only turn as they swing from the top, but as slow-motion analysis proves, your core doesn't "clear" (a passive move to the left to get out of the way). Instead, it leads in the same way a six-footer dunks a basketball: He squats, then explodes out of the squat with his pelvis adding snap power, which is something that the concept of clearing doesn't include. The jumper converts pelvic thrust into elevation, while the golfer converts pelvic thrust into clubhead speed. Firing your pelvis to the right of the target is the key element in the kinematic sequence in which linear and rotational motion combine for a big bang at impact.

—Top 100 Teacher Dr. T.J. Tomasi, Tomasi Golf, Port St. Lucie, Fla.

FINAL FIX

The Quick Way to Improve Your Ballstriking

Get your downswing sequence right for a more powerful impact

*By Top 100 Teacher **BRIAN MANZELLA**, English Turn G.&C.C., New Orleans, La.*

There's only one way to make crisp contact or create any compression on the ball, and that's to swing down from the top in the correct sequence. In a good swing, the hips reach the ball first, then the hands and then the clubhead. Unfortunately, many amateur players do the exact opposite. Follow this simple drill and learn to get it right.

Step 1 Place three balls on an arc, one at impact, another two feet farther along the arc, and a third one two feet ahead of the second ball. Set the arc so that the third ball is even with your left foot.

Step 2 Make a slow-motion swing. Try to get your hips to arrive at the impact ball first, with your hands and clubhead lagging behind.

Step 3 Your hands shouldn't reach the impact ball until your hips (use your belt buckle as a guide) point toward the second ball. If your hands arrive early, you won't get the contact and compression you're searching for.

Step 4 When your hips start pointing at the third ball, your clubhead should finally reach impact. This sequence—hips, hands, club—is the telltale trait of solid ballstriking.

HIPS FIRST
Near impact, the hips are still ahead of the hands and club.

HANDS SECOND
Your hands reach impact only after your hips clear.

CLUBHEAD LAST
The clubhead needs to lag behind your hips and hands.

Scan this photo
to watch a video of this lesson.

Ernie **Els**

Ernie Els's tag as "the Big Easy" certainly fits. Yes, he's a big guy and, yes, his swing looks as smooth as silk. But make no mistake—Ernie hits the ball *hard*. He's the poster child for torque and leverage—the two swing traits that allow you to add power without swinging harder.

Ernie Els looks smooth, but he swings as fast as any power hitter on Tour. His secret? A perfect sequence that produces speed with minimal effort.

STRAIGHT FROM THE SOURCE

Scan this photo *for a one-on-one lesson with Ernie Els.*

Use shoulder power to start the club back. Try to keep the clubhead as low to the ground as possible.

Pin your left biceps to your chest during your takeaway...

...and try to maintain it as you turn your shoulders and complete your backwing.

A lot of amateurs see my swing and assume it's mostly arms because it has good tempo. The truth is that I rarely think about moving my arms at all. I make my best swings when I power the club back with my shoulders. Notice here how I've started the club back but the clubhead is still almost hugging the ground. You can't get that by swinging your arms or hinging your wrists to start your swing.

Making a smooth transition at the top is the result of your body and mind recognizing that your backswing is complete and full. If you stop too soon, your body senses that you haven't built enough power into your backswing, and it then speeds up in a jerky rush. When you overextend your backswing, your body senses that you're too long and steps on the gas.

So how do you know when your backswing is full and complete? For me it's always been when I feel that my left shoulder has gotten behind the ball. When my turn gets to this point I know it's time to start back down. No indecision, no hesitation, no rush. **If your transition isn't as smooth as you want it to be, it's because you never get your left shoulder behind the ball.** When you do, you'll be surprised at how much speed and power you get without swinging any harder.

—PGA Tour player Ernie Els

SKILL PRACTICE

Moving from a wide backswing (straight arms)...

...to a narrow downswing (bent right arm)...

...and back to a wide through-swing is the secret to hitting mammoth drives.

QUICK TIP
Good tempo happens when you save your release for the very last moment. More important: The speed of your driver swing should feel the same as your wedge swing.

Swing Wide-Narrow-Wide for Effortless Power

Blow it by your buddies with this lag-building move

By Top 100 Teacher RON GRING, Magnolia Grove G.C., Mobile, Ala.

To hit better shots and swing with a smoother tempo you need to get the feeling of creating lag in your swing. This means increasing the amount of bend in your right arm during your downswing instead of straightening it prematurely. I describe the proper motion as wide-narrow-wide, meaning you extend your arms on the way up to make your backswing as wide as it can be, then bend your right arm on the way back down (the narrowing part) so you can powerfully straighten it through the impact zone.

GET WIDE As you take the club back, keep your left arm parallel to the ground (*left photo*). This helps you extend both arms during your backswing, which is key to setting them in the right position to create lag and speed on the way down.

GET NARROW From the top, try to re-create your parallel left arm position, but do it while aggressively bending your right elbow (*middle photo*). As you do this, rotate your hips and upper body while pulling your right elbow down.

GET WIDE AGAIN "Crack the whip" by extending both arms as you swing through the ball (*right photo*). This final wide position is what sends your swing speed off the charts. It should feel like you're transferring the energy stored in your bent right elbow to the ball as you straighten both arms through the impact zone. The longer they remain straight, the better.

SKILL ANALYSIS

Scan this photo to see Ernie's swing in pure slow motion.

Els's free-and-easy wrist hinge and right-elbow fold put him perfectly on plane at the top (shaft pointing parallel left of his target).

Ernie's wrists are active going back but passive starting down. His first move is to drop his right elbow down using his right back muscles.

Ernie's left hip is higher than his right. He has pulled it up and to the left using his powerful glutes. His arms and clubhead follow suit.

Once you feel your hands ahead of the ball at impact, copy Els and straighten your arms and release the hinge in your wrists.

The club exits on a plane much like the one it took going back. For best results, point the back of your right hand at the sky during your release.

Els bends his elbows, as if he's throwing the club over his left shoulder. This is a near-perfect follow-through position.

WATCH & LEARN GET "WRISTY" TO IMPROVE YOUR TEMPO

"Be quick, but don't hurry." This famous quote from UCLA coaching legend John Wooden is an apt description for Ernie Els's swing—the clubhead moves quickly, but Ernie is never in a hurry. **Els understands that power comes from proper sequencing, that it builds rather than bursts.** Most golfers confuse good tempo like Els's with swinging slowly, when in fact tempo means to move the club at the same consistent pace throughout your motion.

One of the secrets to generating Els's effortless power is in your wrists. Notice how he hinges them quickly and fully as he swings the club to the top. When he unhinges them on his downswing, it gives the appearance of swinging smoothly, even though his clubhead is blasting through impact at 120 mph.

You should mimic his hinge, but don't copy it move for move. Ernie cups his left wrist at the top and releases the club very late. He does this to fight his tendency to hook the ball under pressure. You'll do better with a flat left wrist at the top and a strong release once your hands reach the hitting zone.
—*Top 100 Teacher Dr. T.J. Tomasi, Tomasi Golf, Port St. Lucie, Fla.*

FINAL FIX

Time Your Swing for a Smoother Release

My full-overlap grip works wonders for tempo and errant shots

*By Top 100 Teacher **MIKE BENDER**, Mike Bender Golf Academy at Magnolia Plantation G.C., Lake Mary, Fla.*

You haven't learned to utilize your forearms and hands properly in your swing, and as a result you're unable to consistently square the clubface as you strike the ball or swing with the correct tempo. More often than not, slices and weak shots are the result. Follow these steps and kiss your slice good-bye.

Step 1 Take your regular grip and slide your right hand up the handle until all the fingers on your right hand overlap those on your left [*frame 1*].

Step 2 Make your swing. As you approach impact use your right hand to pull the knuckles of your left hand down and under [*frames 2–4*].

Step 3 As you swing through impact continue to keep pulling the knuckles under all the way to waist high so that your left wrist stays bowed and your right wrist stays bent backward. As the club moves down through the impact zone, turn your knuckles down toward the ground so your wrists flatten [*frame 5*]. Perform this drill several times without a ball to ingrain the proper feeling.

Turning the knuckles of your left hand toward the ground through impact will keep your slices at bay.

Pro File

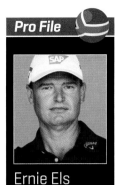

Ernie Els

Full Name Theodore Ernest Els
Nickname The Big Easy
Born October 17, 1969
Birthplace Johannesburg, South Africa
Residence Jupiter, Fla.
Height / Weight 6' 3" / 210 lbs.
College None
Turned professional 1989
Professional victories 65 [19 PGA Tour]*
Majors 1994, 1997 U.S. Open; 2002, 2012 British Open*
Career U.S. earnings $45.6 million*

*Through 2013 U.S. Open

Rank File

PGA Tour Stats

Driving Distance	**294.6 yds.** [51st]
Clubhead Speed	**113.2 mph** [94th]
Driving Accuracy	**56.7%** [155th]
Greens in Regulation	**66.5%** [53rd]

2012 season; courtesy of PGATour.com

Els's Driver

Callaway RAZR Fit Xtreme

Skill No. 23
ALL-AROUND SWING

Adam
Scott

With a major title finally under his belt, Adam Scott is no longer the elite player who has failed to deliver on his promise. Instead, he has improved his swing to the point where it's the most talked about and admired on Tour. Stealing even a few of his moves will make your error-prone full swing a thing a beauty and add yards and accuracy in the process.

From start to finish, Adam Scott rotates around a stable spine to produce one of the most envied swings in golf.

SKILL BREAKDOWN

"Adam Scott is a master at keeping his head steady and his body centered." —Lou Guzzi

Adam Scott is a master at keeping his head steady and his body centered, which in turn gives him the ability to maintain his spine angle during his swing. This is what instructors call "staying in the shot," and Adam does it as well as anyone in the history of the game. It's the reason he has what's considered the best overall swing in the business. He's certainly better at staying in the shot than most amateurs, who tend to slide to both sides and bob up and down throughout the swing. This excess movement negates any chance of rotating around a stable spine, which is how you get max speed.

Lots of people get confused when teachers start talking about "spine angle." What it means is that your core needs to remain stable throughout your swing. **If you stay in your posture, you'll maintain your angles and let your arms swing freely, which will allow you to unleash a powerful strike on the ball.**

To get the feeling of locking down your core, try sucking in your stomach and making practice swings. Turn back and through and try to maintain your stability. End your swing hard on your left side, with your eyes looking at the target and your left leg straight. This means that you've been able to rotate fully around your spine and make a complete body turn while maintaining your balance.

—Top 100 Teacher Lou Guzzi, Talamore C.C., Ambler, Pa.

SKILL PRACTICE

1 Make a nice full turn and load up on your right side...

2 ...then rotate your hips as you squat with your knees. Try to "sit" on the bench.

3 The secret to longer drives is to save as much energy for impact as possible.

Scan this photo to watch a video of this lesson.

QUICK TIP
Tee the ball so that the center of the ball is just below the top of the clubhead. At impact, this will allow you to connect on the sweet spot, just above the center of the clubface.

The True Source of Pure Swing Power

Use this old-but-current trick to gain serious yards with your driver

By Top 100 Teacher LAIRD SMALL, Pebble Beach Golf Academy, Pebble Beach, Calif.

Your shots lack distance because you don't know how to effectively transfer power from the top of your swing to the downward part of your motion. Your faulty move releases much of your energy way too early in the downswing, leaving very little when you actually get to the ball. You need to create—and store—more power as you move down to the impact zone.

Sam Snead was famous for creating effortless power with his driver by squatting down as he moved into impact. Though many of you probably never saw the Slammer hit a shot, you see this move every week during PGA Tour telecasts. It's really not much different from pitching a baseball or hitting a serve in tennis, except that in golf the ball is on the ground instead of above your shoulders. Try my simple power-squat drill and you'll see your power increase in no time.

Step 1 Set a bench or chair behind your left cheek and make your everyday swing. At the top, make sure both knees are flexed (especially the right) and that your hips are closed to the target line (*frame 1*).

Step 2 As you swing down, bend both knees even more and, as you rotate your lower body toward the target, feel like you're sitting down on the bench or chair behind you (*frame 2*). Get this power squat right and you'll feel a lot more spring as you swing into impact.

SKILL ANALYSIS

Scan this photo to see Adam's swing in pure slow motion.

"I prefer a wider stance. It creates a stronger base, which allows me to turn more."

"The relationship between my arms and chest doesn't change during my takeaway."

"The focus of my swing is to turn around my spine while maintaining my address posture."

"You create effortless power when you unwind around a stable spine."

"When I'm swinging my best, my left foot never moves. I can turn right onto it."

WATCH & LEARN ADAM SCOTT'S MASTERFUL MOVES

Adam Scott was his usual big-hitting self in winning the 2013 Masters, outdriving the field by an average of nine yards. Although the man with the eighth-fastest clubhead speed on Tour has said that his power rarely gives him an advantage over his competitors, he did hit 76.4 percent of Augusta National's greens, compared with his 66.6 percent Tour average. Big drives mean shorter approach shots, after all, making it a lot easier to hold greens.

In Scott's words, "Rotation plays a big part in how I create power in my swing. In fact, when I want to improve my swing, I go to the gym as much as the driving range because it's so important for me to maintain my strength and flexibility." When you start your backswing, focus on taking the club away by turning your shoulders while keeping your hips still. Strive for a smooth, one-piece takeaway, and feel like you're turning into the inside of

"I take the club away with my shoulders and feel like I'm turning into the inside of my right leg."

"Make a big shoulder turn and a small arm turn, keeping your hands away from your head."

"I like to go slow from the top. If my hips start getting too fast, I'll close my stance."

"Try to end your swing really hard on your left side."

"Finish with your eyes looking at the target and your left leg straight."

your right leg (You should see wrinkles in your right pants pocket.)

"Easy power starts with a balanced, athletic address," adds Scott. You know you have it when you feel like you can move in any direction—like a linebacker after the ball is snapped—once you sole the club.

Scott's swing is often compared with that of his idol, Greg Norman. **But Adam's technique actually more closely resembles Tiger Woods's form from 2000, both crafted under the tutelage of Butch Harmon (and, in Scott's case, Brad Malone since 2009).** Scott swings on his right-arm plane (ball-through-

biceps line) with massive extension on the takeaway and incredible hip speed through impact. That's vintage Tiger! Add the best setup in golf and you have the perfect recipe for balance and speed. —*Top 100 Teacher Mike Adams, The Medalist Club, Hobe Sound, Fla., and Hamilton Farm G.C., Gladstone, N.J.*

STRAIGHT FROM THE SOURCE

RELAX

A wider stance establishes a stronger base and allows me to turn more, yet remain in balance. Before I grip the club, I relax my arms and let them hang from my shoulders. When they start to feel a bit heavy, that's when I'm ready.

GET SET

Copy Greg Norman, who was my idol growing up. Greg had that nice short backswing that stayed really firm at the top. That's the feeling I wanted and that I still go after—making sure the club isn't flipping around at the top.

BE QUIET

I don't want too much going on from the waist down, especially when driving. On good days, my left foot is solidly planted on the ground as I swing through the hitting zone.

DROP BACK

When your swing starts feeling out of sync, take your normal stance then drop your right foot back. This will restrains your hips from spinning out. It will also give you something more to hit against, and it promotes a right-to-left shot.

SYNC OR SWIM

I like to leave my right heel on the ground a little longer in the downswing. I don't want to hit the ball flat-footed, but I like the feeling of my heel staying on the ground until it rolls up at impact.

FINAL FIX

Use Your Power Circles

Maximize your distance by swinging your hands and clubhead on different paths

By Top 100 Teacher KRISTA DUNTON, Berkeley Hall, Bluffton, S.C.

If you want to knock it straight and long like Adam Scott, you need to make sure your hands and the clubhead are moving on the proper paths. The secret is to swing your hands on a smaller, inner circle both on your backswing and downswing while at the same time keeping the clubhead on a larger, outer circle. To make this happen correctly, concentrate first on your hand path. A common fault is to allow the hands to move to the outside (i.e., away from you) on the downswing in an attempt to create a wider, more powerful swing. This is a huge, power-sapping mistake. Instead, picture a smaller circle or path in your swing and try to keep your hands there throughout your motion (*photo, below*).

Next, picture a larger circle and make this the target for your clubhead throughout your motion. A great way to grasp the right technique is to picture your hands as the hub of a wheel, with the shaft being one of the spokes and the clubhead the outer rim. With this arrangement, your hands will move fast, but the clubhead will race even faster to keep up since it has a larger distance to travel from the top of your backswing to the impact zone.

Pro File

Adam Scott

Full Name Adam Derek Scott
Nickname Scotty
Born July 16, 1980
Birthplace Adelaide, Australia
Residence Crans sur Sierre, Switzerland
Height / Weight 6' 0" / 180 lbs.
College UNLV
Turned professional 2000
Professional victories 21 (9 PGA Tour)*
Majors 2013 Masters*
Career U.S. earnings $30.7 million*

*Through 2013 U.S. Open

Rank File

PGA Tour Stats

Driving Distance
304.6 yds. (10th)

Clubhead Speed
119.3 mph (15th)

Driving Accuracy
59.6% (123rd)

Greens in Regulation
66.6% (50th)

2012 season; courtesy of PGATour.com

Scott's Driver

Titleist 913D3

Yes!

Scan this photo to watch a video of this lesson.

Move your hands on the inner circle and the clubhead on the outer circle to deliver the club on plane.

No!

Swing your hands and clubhead on the inner circle and you'll be too shallow.

No!

Swing your hands and clubhead on the outer plane and you'll be too steep.

Skill No. 24
FUNDAMENTALS

Tiger
Woods

You can't swing like Tiger Woods because no one can—not even the other guys on Tour. What you can do is copy Tiger's rock-solid fundamentals. Like almost everything else in his career, Tiger's famous swing changes are grounded in the proven basics of the game. When Tiger makes an adjustment, it's to fix a tendency he has that strays from those essentials. This consistency has made Tiger the most dominant player of his—and perhaps any—generation.

Tiger Woods has reinvented his swing no less than three times in his career. The effort has resulted in one of the most fundamentally solid swings in history.

SKILL BREAKDOWN

Address Fundamentals

Tiger's swing has changed over the years. Some of the alterations have been made to achieve or correct a certain ballflight, while others have been inserted to accommodate or prevent an injury. Regardless of the state of his swing, Tiger has always set up and swung with great posture. The numbers at right are good ones to emulate, but keep in mind that proper posture at address doesn't matter unless you know how to use it to your advantage. This is where Tiger excels. One of his best power moves is to increase his forward bend during his downswing while elongating his lower body. **At impact, his hips are higher than at address and his knees and ankles are much straighter, but his upper body and head are actually closer to the ball.** When you hear instructors talk about "leveraging the ground" to create speed, this is it. —*Top 100 Teacher Jon Tattersall, Terminus Club, Atlanta, Ga.*

"Regardless of the state of his swing, Tiger has always set up and swung with great posture."

—Jon Tattersall

UPPER BODY

Tiger bends from his hip joints, not from his waist. He also angles his pelvis downward, which helps flatten his lower back. This is commonly known as neutral spine tilt.

BACK

Tiger's upper back isn't flat (nor should it be), and even though he has pulled his shoulders back to widen his chest, his arms hang almost straight down, leaving a gap between his right ear and shoulder.

ARMS

Tiger's arms hang more vertically these days as a result of his increased forward tilt. This makes it easier for him to keep his arms close to his chest when he swings, which negates the need to rotate them as much as he previously had to.

KNEES

Tiger's knees are flexed, not bent. A good checkpoint here is that a line drawn straight down from the front of your right knee intersects the middle of your right big toe.

43°
Angle of Forward Tilt

FLEX FOR POWER

Strong players such as Tiger flex their knees, hips and ankles at address so that they can extend them at contact, just like a basketball player jumping to throw down a dunk.

25°
Knee flex

9°
Ankle bend

SKILL BREAKDOWN

Backswing Fundamentals

Tiger creates a tremendous amount of width in his swing—something you should copy if you want more yards. How does he do it? He starts his backswing turn with a combination of arm and body movement that keeps the club in front of his chest for a long time. Notice in the photos below how far he turns while bringing the club from address to hip height. Already, his back is facing the target, while his arms are still fully extended and the clubhead is in front of his chest. His lower body keeps quiet, and his head stays level even as it turns slightly. You probably don't have Tiger's impressive flexibility, but that doesn't mean you can't make a similar move.

—*Top 100 Teacher Peter Kostis, Kostis-McCord Learning Center, Scottsdale, Ariz.*

No independent moving parts— the ultimate one-piece takeaway.

Clubshaft and left arm moving in same plane.

Left side of torso angled toward ball at the top.

SKILL PRACTICE

Roll and Lift for More Turn

This easy move adds automatic power

Tiger creates great width in his swing with his turn because of his amazing flexibility. (One of his nicknames on Tour is Gumby.) But just because you can't stretch like him, doesn't mean you can't turn like him. You just need to release your left heel, hip and knee more. Keeping your left heel down is not a fundamental of the golf swing, but making the proper turn is. Many players fear lifting their left heel in the backswing because they think they'll sway back and lose control. But that won't happen if you lift your heel correctly. The key is to roll your left foot in while you lift your heel. This allows you to properly release your left knee, which frees up your hips and shoulders to turn fully on the way to the top.

—*Top 100 Teacher Peter Kostis*

Rolling and lifting your left heel allows your left knee, hips and shoulders to make a fuller turn.

No!

Don't just lift up your left heel— you'll sway back when you turn.

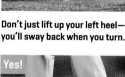

Yes!

Roll your left foot and lift your heel and you'll make a full turn.

SKILL BREAKDOWN

Top Position Fundamentals

Even Tiger has struggled with finding the correct swing plane. To get yours on the right track, place the shaft of any club over your right shoulder and lift your left arm so that the underside of your lead forearm rests on the shaft (*top photo, below*). This is your correct swing plane. Match this checkpoint when you make real swings. —*Top 100 Teacher Peter Kostis, Kostis-McCord Learning Center, Scottsdale, Ariz.*

Find your correct swing plane...

...then match that plane at the top of your backswing.

Club parallel to left arm.

Clubface parallel to left wrist.

Hands as far away from the head as possible.

Right arm folded.

Right shoulder higher than left.

Left arm straight.

Left shoulder under chin.

SKILL BREAKDOWN

Downswing Fundamentals

Although it doesn't look like Tiger's posture changes that much from address to the top, it does. At the top, his left side (not his chest) is tilted toward the ball and his forward bend is nowhere near what it was at address. When you have Tiger's core strength and flexibility, you can pull this off while making it look like you're winding up without changing your angles.

While Tiger slightly increases the tilt in his pelvis going back, he rapidly decreases it during his downswing (5 to 10 degrees). His hips level out and his forward bend toward the ball is close to where it

was at address. It's as though he's doing ab crunches in the gym. The good news? You don't need Tiger's six-pack to make this move.

The secret is in your ankles and feet. Tour players roll **their ankles to shift weight from the right leg to the left.** Tiger is one of the best at this, and not only does he roll his ankles, he actively pushes off the ground from the top of his swing through

impact. This pushing action is real—most big hitters we've tested have at least a 20-inch vertical jump.
—*Top 100 Teacher Jon Tattersall, Terminus Club, Atlanta, Ga.*

SKILL PRACTICE

Hit From Your Toes

Get Tiger's best power move in 10 seconds

You try to create extra speed, but do so mainly with upper-body strength. Not good. You need to make a significant change in your technique or you'll never reach your distance potential

Take Van Halen's advice: *Jump!* Start using the ground as a jumping-off point. Your lower body is your true source of power, as evidenced

by long hitters such as Tiger Woods. Tiger dips down as he starts his downswing, then shoots up onto his toes as he moves through impact. This is exactly what you should do too.

Backswing Shift plenty of weight onto your right side, so much that you can lift your left foot off the ground without losing your balance.

Downswing Flex your legs so that your weight moves slightly down toward the ground—it should feel like you're squatting a bit.

Impact Push off the ground hard as if you're going to jump into the air. You should feel your body weight shoot up rather than straight into the ball and feel as if you're being

Scan this photo *to watch a video of this lesson.*

HEELS UP! Jump into the ball through impact with only your toes touching the ground for maximum power.

pulled up onto your toes through impact. Instant distance, just how Tiger does it.
—*Top 100 Teacher Jon Tattersall*

SKILL BREAKDOWN

Impact Fundamentals

Great ballstrikers "grow" the clubshaft out of their left arm at impact. Here's what I mean: Notice at address how the clubshaft extends straight out from your left forearm. Good ballstrikers such as Tiger re-create this alignment at impact. **The goal is to feel like the club is growing out of your left arm as you strike the ball.** If you can maintain this relationship until the momentum of your swing causes your left arm to fold in your release, you'll hit the ball straight and solidly.

Get a feel for this by developing a stinger swing like Tiger's (*see steps, opposite page*). Think of it as a punch shot with a little extra oomph. When you make contact, try to get the shaft and your left arm to match the positions they held at address. It helps if you "stick" the club at impact. Then work on keeping your left arm and clubshaft in line until your swing moves past your left leg. You'll develop some serious shotmaking skill and improve your swing, to boot.

—Golf Magazine *contributor and NBC lead golf analyst Johnny Miller*

Scan this photo *to see Tiger's swing in pure slow motion.*

Square shoulders turning level to the ground.

Left hip moving to the left and up.

Hands leading the club into impact.

Slightly bowed left wrist.

Clubshaft "growing" out of left arm.

Posted left leg.

Pushing off the ground, shifting weight forward.

Square clubface.

SKILL PRACTICE

Hit Tiger's Stinger

Split fairways and find greens with this target-finding laser

A stinger is a low-flying drive you hit with one of your long irons, or as is the case with Tiger, anything from a pitching wedge to the driver. It's a great shot for when you're hitting into the wind or when you need to be superaccurate on a tight driving hole and you can sacrifice some distance off the tee. —*Top 100 Teacher Mike Lopuszynski, David Glenz Golf Academy, Franklin, N.J.*

Step 1 Set up so that you're slightly in front of the ball. (Your shirt buttons should be just ahead of the ball).

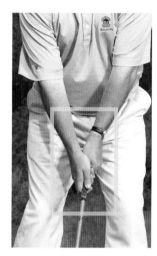

Step 2 Grip down one inch. This allows you to stand closer to the ball, which helps you hit down on it.

Step 3 Make a shoulder-high to shoulder-high swing. The shorter the swing, the lower the ballflight.

Step 4 Lead the clubhead into impact with your hands. Swing at 70 percent—harder swings tend to increase loft.

Step 5 Make sure your left wrist is bowed at impact. This deflofts the club for extra distance.

Step 6 Make a three-quarter follow-though. A full finish fuels a high trajectory, so make sure to cut yours short.

SKILL BREAKDOWN

"Long" arms here.

Spine angle maintained here.

Club exiting out left shoulder here.

"When Tiger has struggled, it's usually due to the club exiting below his left shoulder."

—Jon Tattersall

Release Fundamentals

When Tiger has struggled, it's usually due to the club exiting below his left shoulder. This low exit position indicates that his arms are simply too far away from his body on his downswing. The result is a jammed position reminiscent of a midhandicapper's swing. **When he's on, his exit plane is much higher because his clubhead approaches impact on a shallower angle of attack.** This results in the club extending out away from his body past impact. Tiger also keeps his left foot in the same solid position it held at address. This is key for hitting against a firm left side and producing max power.

The old saying that the quality of any swing position is the result of the positions that preceded it holds especially true for Tiger. Making key fixes in his takeaway and top position over the past seasons have pretty much repaired everything that follows, including his low exit plane. If you're feeling jammed like Tiger does when he's off in your through-swing, try to keep your arms closer to your body on your downswing so they can get farther away from you through impact. Think "long arms" as you move past impact and you'll be on track.
—*Top 100 Teacher Brady Riggs, Woodley Lakes G.C., Van Nuys, Calif.*

FINAL FIX

Trigger a Smooth Release

Here's an easy checkpoint to groove a powerful end to your swing

There are a number of things good players do to create powerful shots, but possibly the most important is fully releasing the club through impact. What this means is that they allow the clubhead to pass their hands as it moves through the hitting zone, a move that releases all the stored power to the ball. If you've noticed how good players look like they're cracking a whip when they swing, this is the reason.

A great trick for improving your release is to use your right index finger as a trigger. At address, separate your right index finger from the rest of your grip when you place your hands on the handle, almost as though you're getting ready to pull the trigger on a gun. If you copy this position, your right hand can exert more pressure on the handle when you swing, making it much easier to turn the club over

(toe rotating past the heel) as you extend your arms through the ball.

With this special hold, make your regular swing and make sure to use pressure from your right index finger to release the club. You'll know you're doing it correctly if you feel as if you're hitting a topspin forehand in tennis, with the knuckles on your left hand pointing toward the ground.

—*Top 100 Teacher Laird Small*

Pro File

Tiger Woods

Full Name Eldrick Tont Woods
Nickname Tiger
Born December 30, 1975
Birthplace Cypress, Calif.
Residence Jupiter Island, Fla.
Height / Weight 6' 1" / 185 lbs.
College Stanford University
Turned professional 1996
Professional victories 105 [78 PGA Tour]*
Majors 1997, 2001, 2002, 2005 Masters; 2000, 2002, 2008 U.S. Open; 2000, 2005, 2006 British Open; 1999, 2000, 2006, 2007 PGA Championship*
Career U.S. earnings $106.9 million*

*Through 2013 U.S. Open

Rank File

PGA Tour Stats

Driving Distance
297.4 yds. [32nd]

Clubhead Speed
120.9 mph [4th]

Driving Accuracy
63.9% [55th]

Greens in Regulation
67.6% [29th]

2012 season; courtesy of PGATour.com

Scan this photo to watch a video of this lesson.

No!
Left-hand knuckles pointing toward the sky.

Yes!
Left-hand knuckles pointing down. Use your right index finger to help turn the club over.

The Top 100 Teachers in America

GOLF MAGAZINE
TOP 100
TEACHERS
IN AMERICA

A quick look at the nation's most exclusive— and talented—team of teaching experts.

SINCE its inception in 1996, *Golf Magazine's* Top 100 Teachers in America list has become the industry standard for instruction excellence, not only because it was the first such list ever created, but because of the diligent selection process that the magazine employs to assemble it. Every other year, we start from scratch in our effort to determine the best 100 teachers in the nation.

The Top 100 list is the only national golf instructor roster that combines outside academic and PGA professional peer review. Candidates for *Golf Magazine's* Top 100 Teachers in America list are selected from nominees submitted by the PGA, LPGA, United States Golf Teachers Federation, top industry executives and readers just like you. More than 250 nominations on average are accepted from the country's 28,000 instruction professionals.

ACTIVE TEACHERS

MIKE ADAMS
Facility: The Medalist Club, Hobe Sound, Fla.; Hamilton Farm G.C., Gladstone, N.J.
Web site: mikeadamsgolf.com
Teaching since: 1977
Top 100 since: 1996

ROB AKINS
Facility: Spring Creek Ranch, Collierville, Tenn.
Web site: robakinsgolf.com
Teaching since: 1987
Top 100 since: 2001

ERIC ALPENFELS
Facility: Pinehurst Resort, N.C.
Web site: pinehurst.com
Teaching since: 1984
Top 100 since: 2001

CHERYL ANDERSON
Facility: Mike Bender Golf Academy at Magnolia Plantation G.C., Lake Mary, Fla.
Web site: mikebender.com
Teaching since: 1995
Top 100 since: 2013
2006 LPGA Teacher of the Year

TODD ANDERSON
Facility: Sea Island Golf Learning Center, St. Simons Island, Ga.
Web site: seaisland.com
Teaching since: 1984
Top 100 since: 2003
2010 PGA Teacher of the Year

MIKE BENDER
Facility: Mike Bender Golf Academy at Magnolia Plantation G.C., Lake Mary, Fla.
Web site: mikebender.com
Teaching since: 1990
Top 100 since: 1996
2009 PGA Teacher of the Year

MIKE BENNETT
Facility: Stack & Tilt Academy, Mount Holly, N.J., and West Palm Beach, Fla.
Web site: stackandtilt.com
Teaching since: 1997
Top 100 since: 2013

MARK BLACKBURN
Facility: Blackburn Golf at The Ledges C.C., Huntsville, Ala.; Gunter's Landing, Guntersville, Ala.
Web site: blackburngolf.com
Teaching since: 1990
Top 100 since: 2013

STEVE BOSDOSH
Facility: Members Club at Four Streams, Beallsville, Md.
Web site: stevebosdoshgolf.com
Teaching since: 1983
Top 100 since: 2001

MICHAEL BREED
Facility: Manhattan Woods G.C., Pearl River, N.Y.
Web site: michaelbreed.com
Teaching since: 1986
Top 100 since: 2003
2012 PGA Teacher of the Year

BRAD BREWER
Facility: Shingle Creek Resort, Orlando, Fla.
Web site: bradbrewer.com
Teaching since: 1984
Top 100 since: 2007

HENRY BRUNTON
Facility: Henry Brunton Golf Academy, Maple, Ont.
Web site: henrybrunton.com
Teaching since: 1985
Top 100 since: 2005

ANNE CAIN
Facility: PGA Tour Academy, World Golf Village, St. Augustine, Fla.
Web site: annecaingolf.com
Teaching since: 1995
Top 100 since: 2013

JASON CARBONE
Facility: Baltusrol G.C., Springfield, N.J.
Teaching since: 1993
Top 100 since: 2007

CHRIS COMO
Facility: Gleneagles C.C., Plano, Tex.
Web site: chriscomogolf.com
Teaching since: 1997
Top 100 since: 2013

CHUCK COOK
Facility: Chuck Cook Golf Academy, Austin, Tex.
Web site: chuckcookgolf.com
Teaching since: 1975
Top 100 since: 1996
1996 PGA Teacher of the Year

DONALD CRAWLEY
Facility: Boulders Golf Academy, Carefree, Ariz.
Web site: golfsimplified.com
Teaching since: 1974
Top 100 since: 1999

MIKE DAVIS
Facility: Walters Golf Academy, Las Vegas, Nev.
Web site: mikedavisgolf.net
Teaching since: 1971
Top 100 since: 2007

GLENN DECK
Facility: Pelican Hill Resort, Newport Beach, Calif.
Web site: pelicanhill.com
Teaching since: 1983
Top 100 since: 2003

DOM DiJULIA
Facility: Jericho National G.C., New Hope, Pa.
Web site: dijuliagolf.com
Teaching since: 1989
Top 100 since: 2007

KRISTA DUNTON
Facility: Berkeley Hall, Bluffton, S.C.
Web site: kristadunton.com
Teaching since: 1989
Top 100 since: 2011
2002 LPGA Teacher of the Year

JOHN ELLIOTT, JR.
Facility: Golden Ocala Golf and Equestrian Club, Ocala, Fla.
Web site: jmegolf.com
Teaching since: 1970
Top 100 since: 1996

CHUCK EVANS
Facility: Gold Canyon Golf Resort, Gold Canyon, Ariz.
Web site: medicusgolfinstitute.com
Teaching since: 1970
Top 100 since: 2009

SEAN FOLEY
Facility: Core Golf Academy, Windermere, Fla.
Web site: coregolfacademy.com
Teaching since: 1995
Top 100 since: 2013

EDEN FOSTER
Facility: Maidstone Club, East Hampton, N.Y.
Teaching since: 1988
Top 100 since: 2003

BRYAN GATHRIGHT
Facility: Oak Hills C.C., San Antonio, Tex.
Teaching since: 1987
Top 100 since: 2001

GARY GILCHRIST
Facility: Gary Gilchrist Golf Academy, Howey-in-the-Hills, Fla.
Web site: gggolf.com
Teaching since: 1990
Top 100 since: 2013

DAVID GLENZ
Facility: David Glenz Golf Academy, Franklin, N.J.
Web site: davidglenz.com
Teaching since: 1978
Top 100 since: 1996
1998 PGA Teacher of the Year

RICK GRAYSON
Facility: Rivercat G.C., Springfield, Mo.
Web site: rickgraysongolf.com
Teaching since: 1976
Top 100 since: 1996

FRED GRIFFIN
Facility: Grand Cypress Academy of Golf, Orlando, Fla.
Web site: grandcypress.com
Teaching since: 1980
Top 100 since: 1996

RON GRING
Facility: Gring Golf at Magnolia Grove G.C., Mobile, Ala.
Web site: gringgolf.com
Teaching since: 1978
Top 100 since: 2003

LOU GUZZI
Facility: Lou Guzzi Golf Academy, Talamore C.C., Ambler, Pa.
Web site: louguzzi.com
Teaching since: 1992
Top 100 since: 2011

MARK HACKETT
Facility: Old Palm G.C., Palm Beach Gardens, Fla.
Teaching since: 1988
Top 100 since: 2009

MARTIN HALL
Facility: Ibis Golf & C.C., West Palm Beach, Fla.
Teaching since: 1978
Top 100 since: 1996
2008 PGA Teacher of the Year

JOE HALLETT
Facility: Vanderbilt Legends Club, Franklin, Tenn.
Web site: pgaguy.com
Teaching since: 1990
Top 100 since: 2011

HANK HANEY
Facility: Hank Haney Golf, McKinney, Tex.
Web site: hankhaney.com
Teaching since: 1977
Top 100 since: 1996

JIM HARDY
Facility: Jim Hardy Golf, Houston, Tex.
Web site: jimhardygolf.com
Teaching since: 1966
Top 100 since: 1996
2007 PGA Teacher of the Year

BILL HARMON
Facility: Toscana C.C., Indian Wells, Calif.
Web site: toscanacc.com
Teaching since: 1970
Top 100 since: 2013

BUTCH HARMON
Facility: Butch Harmon School of Golf, Henderson, Nev.
Web site: butchharmon.com
Teaching since: 1965
Top 100 since: 1996

CRAIG HARMON
Facility: Oak Hill C.C., Rochester, N.Y.
Teaching since: 1968
Top 100 since: 1996

MICHAEL HEBRON
Facility: Smithtown Landing G.C., Smithtown, N.Y.
Web site: mikehebron.com
Teaching since: 1967
Top 100 since: 1996
1991 PGA Teacher of the Year

SHAWN HUMPHRIES
Facility: Cowboys G.C., Grapevine, Tex.
Web site: shawnhumphries.com
Teaching since: 1988
Top 100 since: 2005

ED IBARGUEN
Facility: Duke University G.C., Durham, N.C.
Web site: golf.duke.edu
Teaching since: 1979
Top 100 since: 2001

ERIC JOHNSON
Facility: Oakmont C.C., Oakmont, Pa.
Web site: ericjohnsongolf.com
Teaching since: 1991
Top 100 since: 2011

CHARLIE KING
Facility: Reynolds Golf Academy, Greensboro, Ga.
Web site: reynoldsgolfacademy.com
Teaching since: 1989
Top 100 since: 2003

JERRY KING
Facility: Jerry King Golf Academy, Lahaina, Maui, Hawaii
Web site: jerrykinggolf.com
Teaching since: 1992
Top 100 since: 2009

KEVIN KIRK
Facility: The Woodlands C.C., The Woodlands, Tex.
Web site: thewoodlandscc.com
Teaching since: 1990
Top 100 since: 2013

PETER KOSTIS
Facility: Kostis-McCord Learning Center, Scottsdale, Ariz.
Web site: kostismccordlearning.com
Teaching since: 1971
Top 100 since: 1996

PETER KRAUSE
Facility: Hank Haney Academy, Lewisville, Tex.
Web site: peterkrausegolf.com
Teaching since: 1981
Top 100 since: 1999
2005 PGA Teacher of the Year

MIKE LaBAUVE
Facility: Westin Kierland Resort, Scottsdale, Ariz.
Web site: kierlandresort.com
Teaching since: 1980
Top 100 since: 1996

JAMES LEITZ
Facility: Pinewood C.C., Slidell, La.
Web site: leitzgolf.com
Teaching since: 1982
Top 100 since: 2013

ROD LIDENBERG
Facility: Prestwick G.C., Woodbury, Minn.
Web site: pgamasterpro.com
Teaching since: 1972
Top 100 since: 2007

JACK LUMPKIN
Facility: Sea Island Golf Learning Center, St. Simons Island, Ga.
Web site: seaisland.com
Teaching since: 1958
Top 100 since: 1996
1995 PGA Teacher of the Year

KEITH LYFORD
Facility: Old Greenwood G.C., Truckee, Calif.
Web site: lyfordgolf.net
Teaching since: 1982
Top 100 since: 1999

DALE LYNCH
Facility: BannLynch Golf at Saddlebrook Resort, Tampa, Fla.
Web site: bannlynchgolf.com
Teaching since: 1988
Top 100 since: 2013

TIM MAHONEY
Facility: Talking Stick G.C., Scottsdale, Ariz.
Web site: timmahoneygolf.com
Teaching since: 1980
Top 100 since: 1996

MIKE MALASKA
Facility: Superstition Mountain G.C., Superstition Mountain, Ariz.
Web site: malaskagolf.com
Teaching since: 1982
Top 100 since: 1996
2011 PGA Teacher of the Year

BRIAN MANZELLA
Facility: English Turn Golf & C.C., New Orleans, La.
Web site: brianmanzella.com
Teaching since: 1989
Top 100 since: 2011

PAUL MARCHAND
Facility: Shadowhawk G.C., Richmond, Tex.
Teaching since: 1981
Top 100 since: 1996

RICK McCORD
Facility: McCord Golf Academy at Orange Lake C.C., Orlando, Fla.
Web site: themccordgolfacademy.com
Teaching since: 1973
Top 100 since: 1996

MIKE McGETRICK
Facility: McGetrick Golf, Spartanburg. S.C..
Teaching since: 1983
Top 100 since: 1996
1999 PGA Teacher of the Year

JIM McLEAN
Facility: McLean Golf, Miami, Fla.
Web site: jimmclean.com
Teaching since: 1975
Top 100 since: 1996
1994 PGA Teacher of the Year

BRIAN MOGG
Facility: Waldorf Astoria G.C., Orlando, Fla.
Web site: moggperformance.com
Teaching since: 1992
Top 100 since: 2005

BILL MORETTI
Facility: Moretti Golf, Austin, Tex.
Web site: morettigolf.com
Teaching since: 1979
Top 100 since: 1996

SCOTT MUNROE
Facility: Nantucket G.C., Siasconset, Mass.
Web site: moneygolf.net
Teaching since: 1978
Top 100 since: 2009

JIM MURPHY
Facility: Sugar Creek C.C., Sugar Land, Tex.
Web site: jimmurphygolf.com
Teaching since: 1984
Top 100 since: 2003

TOM NESS
Facility: Reunion G.C., Hoschton, Ga.
Web site: affinitigolfacademy.com
Teaching since: 1972
Top 100 since: 2007

CHRIS O'CONNELL
Facility: Plane Truth Golf Institute, Plano, Tex.
Web site: planetruthgolf.com
Teaching since: 1997
Top 100 since: 2013

DAVE PELZ
Facility: Pelz Golf, Austin, Tex.
Web site: pelzgolf.com
Teaching since: 1976
Top 100 since: 1996

MIKE PERPICH
Facility: RiverPines G.C., Johns Creek, Ga.
Web site: mikeperpich.com
Teaching since: 1980
Top 100 since: 2001

GALE PETERSON
Facility: Sea Island Golf Learning Center, St. Simons Island, Ga.
Web site: seaisland.com
Teaching since: 1978
Top 100 since: 1996
1996 LPGA Teacher of the Year

E.J. PFISTER
Facility: Oak Tree National, Edmond, Okla.
Web site: ejpfistergolf.com
Teaching since: 1986
Top 100 since: 2009

DAVE PHILLIPS
Facility: TPI, Oceanside, Calif.
Web site: mytpi.com
Teaching since: 1989
Top 100 since: 2001

ANDY PLUMMER
Facility: Stack & Tilt Academy, Mount Holly, N.J., and West Palm Beach, Fla.
Web site: stackandtilt.com
Teaching since: 1997
Top 100 since: 2013

CAROL PREISINGER
Facility: The Kiawah Island Club, Kiawah Island, S.C.
Web site: carolpreisinger.com
Teaching since: 1986
Top 100 since: 2005

KIP PUTERBAUGH
Facility: The Aviara Golf Academy, Carlsbad, Calif.
Web site: aviaragolfacademy.com
Teaching since: 1972
Top 100 since: 1996

NANCY QUARCELINO
Facility: Kings Creek G.C., Spring Hill, Tenn.
Web site: qsog.com
Teaching since: 1979
Top 100 since: 2003
2000 LPGA Teacher of the Year

DANA RADER
Facility: Ballantyne Resort, Charlotte, N.C.
Web site: danarader.com
Teaching since: 1980
Top 100 since: 1996
1990 LPGA Teacher of the Year

BRADY RIGGS
Facility: Woodley Lakes G.C., Van Nuys, Calif.
Web site: bradyriggs.com
Teaching since: 1990
Top 100 since: 2007

DON SARGENT
Facility: Scioto C.C., Columbus, Ohio
Web site: sciotocc.com
Teaching since: 1990
Top 100 since: 2013

ADAM SCHRIBER
Facility: Crystal Mountain Resort, Thompsonville, Mich.
Web site: crystalmountain.com
Teaching since: 1985
Top 100 since: 2009

CRAIG SHANKLAND
Facility: LPGA International, Daytona Beach, Fla.
Teaching since: 1957
Top 100 since: 1996
2001 PGA Teacher of the Year

MIKE SHANNON
Facility: Sea Island Golf Learning Center, St. Simons Island, Ga.
Web site: seaisland.com
Teaching since: 1975
Top 100 since: 1996

TED SHEFTIC
Facility: Bridges G.C., Abbottstown, Pa.
Web site: tedsheftic.com
Teaching since: 1966
Top 100 since: 2003

JAMES SIECKMANN
Facility: Shadow Ridge C.C., Omaha, Nebr.
Web site: jsegolfacademy.com
Teaching since: 1991
Top 100 since: 2013

LAIRD SMALL
Facility: Pebble Beach Golf Academy, Pebble Beach, Calif.
Web site: pebblebeach.com
Teaching since: 1977
Top 100 since: 1996
2003 PGA Teacher of the Year

KEVIN SMELTZ
Facility: David Leadbetter Golf Academy, Champions Gate, Fla.
Web site: davidleadbetter.com
Teaching since: 1998
Top 100 since: 2013

RANDY SMITH
Facility: Royal Oaks C.C., Dallas, Tex.
Teaching since: 1973
Top 100 since: 2001
2002 PGA Teacher of the Year

RICK SMITH
Facility: Treetops Resort, Gaylord, Mich.
Web site: ricksmith.com
Teaching since: 1977
Top 100 since: 1996

TODD SONES
Facility: Impact Golf Schools at White Deer Run G.C., Vernon Hills, Ill.
Web site: toddsones.com
Teaching since: 1982
Top 100 since: 1996

MITCHELL SPEARMAN
Facility: Isleworth Golf & C.C., Windermere, Fla.; Doral Arrowwood Golf Resort, Rye Brook, N.Y.
Web site: mitchellspearman.com
Teaching since: 1979
Top 100 since: 1996

MARK STEINBAUER
Facility: Carlton Woods, The Woodlands, Tex.
Teaching since: 1977
Top 100 since: 2011

KELLIE STENZEL
Facility: Palm Beach G.C., Palm Beach, Fla.
Web site: kelliestenzelgolf.com
Teaching since: 1990
Top 100 since: 2009

TOM STICKNEY
Facility: Bighorn G.C., Palm Desert, Calif.; Promontory G.C., Park City, Utah
Web site: tomstickneygolf.com
Teaching since: 1990
Top 100 since: 2007

DR. JIM SUTTIE
Facility: TwinEagles, Naples, Fla.; Cog Hill G.C., Lemont, Ill.
Web site: jimsuttie.com
Teaching since: 1972
Top 100 since: 1996
2000 PGA Teacher of the Year

JON TATTERSALL
Facility: Terminus Club, Atlanta, Ga.
Web site: terminusclub.com
Teaching since: 1988
Top 100 since: 2007

DR. T.J. TOMASI
Facility: Tomasi Golf, Port St. Lucie, Fla.
Web site: tjtomasi.com
Teaching since: 1975
Top 100 since: 1999

KEVIN WEEKS
Facility: Cog Hill Golf & C.C., Lemont Ill.
Web site: kevinweeks.com
Teaching since: 1990
Top 100 since: 2013

DR. DAVID WRIGHT
Facility: Wright Balance Golf Academy at Arroyo Trabuco G.C., Mission Viejo, Calif.
Web site: wrightbalance.com
Teaching since: 1982
Top 100 since: 2005

JOSH ZANDER
Facility: Zander Golf, at Stanford University G.C., Palo Alto, Calif., and Presidio G.C., San Francisco, Calif.
Web site: zandergolf.com
Teaching since: 1994
Top 100 since: 2013

FEATURED ALUMNI

MIKE LOPUSZYNSKI
Facility: David Glenz Golf Academy, Franklin, N.J.
Web site: glenzgolf.com
Teaching since: 1987
Active Top 100: 1996–2011

BRUCE PATTERSON
Facility: Butler National G.C., Oak Brook, Ill.
Teaching since: 1980
Active Top 100: 2001–2013

SCOTT SACKETT
Facility: Scott Sackett Golf, Scottsdale, Ariz.
Web site: scottsackett.com
Teaching since: 1985
Active Top 100: 1999–2013

CHUCK WINSTEAD
Facility: University Club, Baton Rouge, La.
Web site: universityclubbr.com
Teaching since: 1993
Active Top 100: 2005–2013

WORLD GOLF TEACHERS HALL OF FAME

PEGGY KIRK BELL
Facility: Pine Needles, Southern Pines, N.C.
Teaching since: 1958
1961 LPGA Teacher of the Year

MANUEL DE LA TORRE
Facility: Milwaukee C.C., River Hills, Wis.
Web site: manueldelatorregolf.com
Teaching since: 1948
1986 PGA Teacher of the Year

DAVID LEADBETTER
Facility: David Leadbetter Golf Academy, Champions Gate, Fla.
Web site: davidleadbetter.com
Teaching since: 1976

EDDIE MERRINS
Facility: Bel-Air C.C., Los Angeles, Calif.
Web site: eddiemerrins.com
Teaching since: 1957

BOB TOSKI
Facility: Toski-Battersby Learning Center, Coconut Creek, Fla.
Web site: learn-golf.com
Teaching since: 1956

DR. GARY WIREN
Facility: Trump International, West Palm Beach, Fla.
Web site: garywiren.com
Teaching since: 1955
1987 PGA Teacher of the Year

Top 100 by the Numbers

The Top 100 Organization includes 100 active members of the Top 100 Teachers in America list, 70 alumni and six living members of *Golf Magazine's* World Golf Teachers Hall of Fame. Eleven former Top 100 Teachers have passed, including instruction legend Jim Flick in November 2012. Mr. Flick was inducted into the World Golf Teachers Hall of Fame, created and managed by the Top 100 Teachers in America, in 2000.

92/8 Number of men and women among the active group.

33 Number of teachers who have been on the list every year since 1996.

26 States represented (one teacher instructs in Canada). Florida boasts 19 members, Texas is home to 13, and California is home to 9.

33 Percentage of active members who have been on the list for four years or less, indicating *Golf Magazine's* emphasis on locating emerging talent.

4 Number (in millions) of lessons the teachers have given as a group.

27 Average number of years of teaching experience.

200 Average amount (in dollars) it will cost you for an hour-long lesson with a Top 100 Teacher.

GOLF.com

Get more information on GOLF Magazine's Top 100 Teachers and the Top Teachers by region, plus exclusive video tips and drills at www.golf.com.

Publisher
JIM CHILDS

V.P., Brand and Digital Strategy
STEVEN SANDONATO

Executive Director, Marketing Services
CAROL PITTARD

Executive Director, Retail and Special Sales
TOM MIFSUD

Executive Publishing Director
JOY BUTTS

Director, Bookazine Development and Marketing
LAURA ADAM

Finance Director
GLENN BUONOCORE

Associate Publishing Director
MEGAN PEARLMAN

Assistant General Counsel
HELEN WAN

Assistant Director, Special Sales
ILENE SCHREIDER

Senior Book Production Manager
SUSAN CHODAKIEWICZ

Design and Prepress Manager
ANNE-MICHELLE GALLERO

Brand Manager
MICHELE BOVÉ

Associate Prepress Manager
ALEX VOZNESENSKIY

Assistant Brand Manager
STEPHANIE BRAGA

Editorial Director
STEPHEN KOEPP

SPECIAL THANKS

Katherine Barnet, Virgil Bastos,
Jeremy Biloon, Shaw Burrows, Rose Cirrincione,
Caroline DeNunzio, Davey DeNunzio,
Dominick DeNunzio, Harvey Ewen,
Jacqueline Fitzgerald, Christine Font,
Jenna Goldberg, Hillary Hirsch, David Kahn,
Amy Mangus, Kimberly Marshall, Michael McGuffin,
Nina Mistry, Terry Rowles, Dave Rozzelle,
Ricardo Santiago, Carmel Sweeney,
Adriana Tierno, Vanessa Wu

EDITORIAL

Managing Editor
DAVID M. CLARKE

Creative Director
PAUL CRAWFORD

Executive Editor
CONNELL BARRETT

Editor
DAVID DeNUNZIO (INSTRUCTION),
ROB SAUERHAFT (EQUIPMENT),
GARY PERKINSON (PRODUCTION)

Senior Editor
ALAN BASTABLE

Deputy Editor (Instruction and Equipment)
MICHAEL CHWASKY

Senior Writers
MICHAEL BAMBERGER, CAMERON MORFIT,
ALAN SHIPNUCK, GARY VAN SICKLE

Senior Editor (Travel/Course Rankings)
JOE PASSOV

Digital Production Manager
KAITLIN SANTANNA

Assistant Editor
JESSICA MARKSBURY

Contributing Writers
BRANDEL CHAMBLEE, JOHN GARRITY,
PETER KOSTIS, PAUL MAHONEY, JACK McCALLUM,
JOHNNY MILLER, JOSH SENS

ART

Art Director
PAUL EWEN

Deputy Art Director
KAREN HA

Assistant Photo Editor
JESSE REITER

Imaging
GEOFFREY A. MICHAUD (DIRECTOR, *SI* IMAGING),
GERALD BURKE, NEAL CLAYTON, DAN LARKIN

Contributing Photographers
ANGUS MURRAY, SCHECTER LEE

Contributing Illustrator
GRAHAM GACHES

Technical and Short Game Consultant
DAVE PELZ

Contributing Teachers
THE TOP 100 TEACHERS IN AMERICA 2013-2014
(DR. T.J. TOMASI, PROGRAM DIRECTOR)

Publisher
DICK RASKOPF

**Associate Publisher,
Golf Equipment/Business Development**
BRAD J. FELENSTEIN

Manager, Golf Equipment/Business Development
GARTH ROGERS

Executive Assistant
DELIA LEAHY

TIME INC. SPORTS GROUP

Editor, Time Inc. Sports Group
PAUL FICHTENBAUM

Managing Editor, Sports Illustrated
CHRISTIAN STONE

Managing Editor, SI.com
MATT BEAN

Editor, SI Golf Group
DAVID M. CLARKE

President, Time Inc. Sports Group
MARK FORD

V.P., Publisher
FRANK WALL

Senior V.P., Consumer Marketing
NATE SIMMONS

Senior V.P., Finance
ELISSA FISHMAN

V.P., Communications and Development
SCOTT NOVAK

**Associate Publisher, Marketing and
Creative Services**
CHARLIE SAUNDERS

V.P., Finance
PETER GREER

V.P. and General Manager, Digital
JIM DeLORENZO

V.P., Consumer Marketing
ANN MARIE DOHERTY

V.P., Operations
ROBERT KANELL

Deputy General Counsel
JUDITH MARGOLIN

Human Resources, Executive Director
ALI DEBIASI-INTRES

GOLF.com

Managing Editor
EAMON LYNCH

Assistant Managing Editor
MIKE WALKER

Senior Producers
RYAN REITERMAN, JEFF RITTER

Staff Producer
KEVIN CUNNINGHAM

Play Like a PRO

Words
The Top 100 Teachers in America
with
DAVID DeNUNZIO

Additional reporting by Michael Chwasky,
Jessica Marksbury and Mike Walker

Design
PAUL EWEN

Photography
ANGUS MURRAY,
SCHECTER LEE (EQUIPMENT)

Copy Editor
DON ARMSTRONG

Video Production
OPTIMISM MEDIA GROUP

Contributing Photography
Robert Beck/*SI*: 112 (TR), 128
(Johnson), 138–139, 143 (TR)
Bridgestone Golf: 106 (TR)
Frederic J. Brown/Getty Images: 180 (R)
Simon Bruty/*SI*: 116–117, 126 (L)
Darren Carroll/*SI*: 82–83
Curtis Compton/*Atlanta Journal-*
Constitution: 104–105
D² Productions: 179 (BR), 180 (BL)
Stuart Franklin/Getty Images:
Cover, 66–67, 70, 74 (L)
Scott Halleran/Getty Images: 106 (L)
Kohjiro Kinno/*SI*: 84 (L), 112 (L)
Jason LaVeris/FilmMagic: 185 (TR)
Mark Newcombe/Visions in Golf:
48–49 (sequence), 56–57 (sequence),
158, 160, 172–173, 178, 179 (Woods), 184
Jeff Newton: 126 (TR)
Jon Paterson: 4, 10–11, 42–43, 60–61,
136–137
Andrew Reddington/Getty Images:
68 (L), 168–169
Carlos M. Saavedra/*SI*: 114, 124–125
Marc Serota/*SI*: 88
Jamie Squire/Getty Images: 54 (TR)
Al Tielemans/*SI*: 132 (L), 134
Rob Tringali: 175 (TR)
Ben Van Hook: 68 (TR)
Fred Vuich/SI: 54 (L), 108 (L), 140, 142